PICTURES ON THE PAVEMENT

To

MY PAT

PICTURES ON THE PAVEMENT

by G. W. Stonier

*Illustrated by
Edward Ardizzone*

London

MICHAEL JOSEPH

First published by
MICHAEL JOSEPH LTD
26 Bloomsbury Street
*London, W.C.*1
1955

Set and printed in Great Britain by Unwin Brothers Ltd., at the
Gresham Press, Woking, in Perpetua type, thirteen point leaded,
on paper made by Henry Bruce at Currie in Scotland and bound by
James Burn at Esher

Contents

Acknowledgment

Most of these pieces have appeared in the pages of 'Punch' and 'The New Statesman and Nation'. To the Proprietors of these journals I am indebted for permission to reprint.

The drawings for *Meet at the Widow's*, *The Enchanted Park*, *Crayfish*, *Queues Without End*, *The Art of the Pub Crawl*, *Girls! Girls!*, *No Pipes at the Prom*, *All Perfectly Legal*, *Swan Reach*, and *Stranger*, *Pause* are also reproduced by permission of the Proprietors of 'Punch'.

Paradise Lost

HO could resist, once or twice a year, slipping off to the Zoo? Over the tree tops come the playground voices that aren't quite voices: a too progressive school, perhaps, exercising the Id with whoops, roars, yawns, shrieks and trills. We hurry a little, so as not to miss anything. But there waits the vulture. From his iron dome, hunched, bald, he has marked us; dreadfully he overlooks us as we approach, as we join the trickle of those who, thumbing their half-crowns and shillings, would picnic with Creation. We have come early, though never early enough. Into Eden one should take a solitary way. The first there have been free to wander and interrogate, to eavesdrop, to encounter possibly the Snake up the Apple-tree or (as once came my way) four wolves bounding along a side-walk, reined by the old Fellow who gives them their morning run. But could he hold them? Rather to my surprise, it was they, not I, who crept under a seat.

Today, the show is in full swing. Goats chase children in the corner reserved for them, rides of all sorts are being given, bears wave and Fellows in deck-chairs nod, the elephant bowing left and right like a queen accepts tips, the camel refrains from spitting, and whole families can't resist aping the ape. Oh, how delectably, how frightfully we are interwound! Where can one draw a line?

Has Leo—at this moment stretched asleep while starlings pick at his bone—grown as tired as he looks of being British? Does the lawyer call the fox sly? On which side of the bars do hyenas make up, does the hog snort off in his sports car? Which is the prouder, and which with the more reason, the peacock or I? And when on all sides our atom bombs have been piled and dropped, who will invade—the ant? Here he is under a magnifying lens, on the march, fording rivers, constructing cities. Baffled, he never pauses. Stakhanovism is in his blood, and he may yet inherit the earth. Dread him.

Meanwhile the lords and ladies of creation chew popcorn and have their own favourites, chief among them that sad comedian the bear (where's Brumas now?—slippering in an alley of lost fame), and the whole cartload of monkeys. *They* survive anything, even the unhappy association, for so many poster years, with soap. Advertisement points a ghostly finger, so that we can't squint up a tree at the panda without thinking that he should be under a beach sunshade drinking rum, and the elephant shocks by having forgotten, apparently, the only fountain-pen. The Guinness glass rises everywhere. Seals, pelicans, toucans (one of these, proprietorially adopted), kinkajous: what next? One may have fears for the pretty whydah bird, and the okapi, looking round out of a shy, velvety seclusion, seems to need protection.

Humanity oozes. Some amiable small creatures I tickle, knowing that they will never cadge at me from Tube platforms. The long-nosed 'Diane,' a coati set rather unfairly next to two elegant lemurs, has all the sweetness of nature that may go with sensitive ugly looks: her babes, if any, won't share the honours with Royalty. And others tickle me, especially the young bison who thinks himself Orson Welles and the plated rhino with her drawers slipping down. Tortoises have always been my diversion, partly no doubt from the fascination of seeing so many John D. Rockefellers disporting themselves about a lawn with a palsied immortality all but within their grasp. While I am staring at one great-grandfather, I suddenly realize its hurry. Another centenarian, equally distant, has started for the same lettuce leaf. They are, paralytically, sprinting. This discovery throws me off my timetrack and on to theirs. The days flicker by like a book read; instantly the sun rises, shadows race over the lawn, summer succeeds to spring, autumn to summer; and in the same realization I see the mayfly which grows up, hungers, sports, weds, breeds, and dies, all in a daylight. I think I might even stop going to zoos, which exude boredom, if it weren't that despite everything—despite bars, stench,

litter—Nature will out. The great gaze of the sea-eagle
still holds skies and seas, birds of paradise rend a tapestry
with their mating cry, deer in the open convey shade, and
the upside-down fly, all eye-lashes, moves in a crystal ball
of vision. Here, if anywhere, is Eden.

My particular reason for visiting again the London
Zoo—one of the best-stocked, if not the most beautiful,
of zoos—was to convey to the aquarium a gift of Siamese
fighting fish, which my wife had bred and I lugged. This
earned us a behind-the-scenes tour. We peered at baby
sea-horses, mere hairs with the chess-knight look; we had
our fingers gobbled at by a throng of jumping carp; we
watched the puffer fish swell himself into a football with
water or air according to the element in which he found
himself threatened. One interest of fish is that they enjoy
an existence as ceremonious and as foreign to our own as a
Tibetan monk's. They are they, I am I. I don't have to feel
sorry for them; and that liberation accompanies me as,
walking away across Regent's Park, I hear the shudders of
the Himalayan tiger driven to bed with a hose.

While You Wait

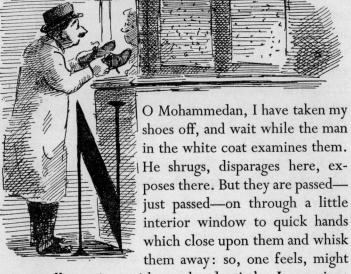

O Mohammedan, I have taken my shoes off, and wait while the man in the white coat examines them. He shrugs, disparages here, exposes there. But they are passed—just passed—on through a little interior window to quick hands which close upon them and whisk them away: so, one feels, might some small cousin vanish at the dentist's. I am given a ticket. I walk on cold lino to an old cinema-seat, one of a dozen; there to wait, muffled, hatted, gloved, but in stockinged feet.

Not that, shoeless myself, I lack shoes for company. In hundreds, along shelf upon shelf to the ceiling, they congregate: shoes sharp and snug, glad shoes, valiant shoes, slippery shoes, shoes that have lost their shine and shoes with a kick in them. They begin dancing, to the thrum and drub of some engine in the background. My own feet discover a hassock. Outside it's raining—which, of course, brought me here.

Ah, it rains (look at it there in the window), and a wet monotony dims distances and silkily opens the pavement at our feet. We feel a new moisture and sap rise in us; *our* pipes are running, *our* gutters sing; and windy arpeggios sweep us from top to toe. Drizzle, drizzle, drizzle; pour, pour, pour. The roads become rivers, buses splash, umbrellas huddle, hats and horses droop, people scatter for doorways, collide, or hover on stilts, while indoors the coals spit and long faces grow longer. Part of me—that impetuous eye which so often overrules feebler senses—may rejoice. But now comes disillusion. My shoe leaks! The cold squelch of one foot (never both) renders action and thought, life itself, intolerable. There's nothing for it but—weighing discomforts—to make for the nearest while-you-wait shop.

Others join me. The shaven-headed man with bare knees, blue belted macintosh, yellow silk scarf, zip bag—a youth leader, no doubt, of some recondite order—having yielded up hobnail clumpers sits at my back where, if I look round, he meets me with circular stares. A fat little lady bobs in with umbrella a-twirl and one heel a-dangling. Should I give up my hassock? While I am pondering this, she fetches slippers out of the *Daily Mirror*, settles in the first to enjoy the second. From time to time a boots whistles in to be told, 'Not yet': some hotel-bound client must be hopping mad to vacate his bedroom before noon.

Meanwhile the jolly reverberations (not unlike those which lap the glass room at a printing works) have increased till the whole shop joins in. Shoes shuffle, the fat lady joggles, the grim scout holds tight; my attention wavers over various Compensation Acts and Warnings of Apparent Death which embellish the walls. Gusts of hammering, faint gluey smells waft over us. Then some new apparatus with a whirr comes into play.

An appalling scream rends the air.

Quite unperturbed, the lady has got up, to receive her shoes, and trot away, umbrella point first, into the wet.

Soon afterwards the mountaineer, monk, Martian— whatever he may be—is beckoned to the counter, and he too, iron-footed, departs, leaving me alone.

Scream follows scream, each more dreadful than the last. It is—it can only be—the voice of the shoe. I should never have come here! Too late. All round me, quite still now, are the shoes waiting. The women's seem to be standing outside hotel bedrooms, the men's are packed ready. Leather has worked hard, rubber has jaunted, crocodile is a cad; and here are high heels and none, soles saved, toes curling, tongues hanging out. What a strange and in the end desolating variety! How tired they look, how empty and cold! For some this will have been the last convalescence; they'll be worn out, chucked away; destitution will be theirs, that terrible solitude which at last must overtake all plodders, divide all pairs. Does the world contain a more tragic spectacle than the *single* shoe, met halfway across a field or on a sea-shore? What comes to its fellow, struggling on till it, too, must rest in its tracks?

Then through the little window my shoes return: altered, shocked, blunted, but still mine. They have died, to be born again. I pay eleven and sixpence, step into them, encountering new hardnesses. Gradually they will warm to me. And outside in the street, where I wade into the first puddle for sheer pleasure, the rain is turning to snow. Snow! My eye leaps, and I resume where I left off.

MEET AT THE WIDOW'S

ALF an age it seemed, though it can't have been more than a few moments. I sat on a sofa at Madame Tussaud's, where, having arranged to meet friends, I had arrived early.

People—mostly in families—were coming and going, drawn into circulation up a staircase, and expelled from the depths through a side door. Those on the way out had gone the whole hog in wax—sailed along its heavens, plumbed its hells—though to look at them you might not have thought so. The same grudging acceptance seemed to characterize all faces, including, no doubt, my own.

Somebody having obligingly left a programme, I was able, without budging an inch, to renew my acquaintance with Groups Royal and Ecclesiastical, Ministers Historic and Ministers Humdrum, the Scout Movement, the Plantagenets, the Mannings, and others as worthy. Still over Mary Queen of Scots the black executioner lifts his axe, the peculiar horror of the occasion being that it's *indoors*, with several onlookers seated on chairs and a fireplace in the background; then, more happily, the Sleeping Lady from Versailles breathes ever with that visible rise and fall which is the inspiration of all; Mahatma Gandhi blinks—no that's an exaggeration—looks mildly surprised to find himself, with Wilberforce, Nurse Cavell, and others, on a tour of Westminster Abbey; they haven't apparently tired of asking that lad with his hands behind him, 'And when did you last see your father?'; Napoleon, impressively, lies dead, but also, grown erect, tall, and handsome, stands by Madame Tussaud herself, the little black widow with a frill cap at whom, with her dreams all come true, we shall look twice; Stalin makes us distrust all chauffeurs, Chaplin is a trapped rat, Winston rises with an ogreish leer; but these, I think, reflect less satire than the failure to achieve likeness. The standard isn't high. If, without reference to the list we can exclaim 'Isn't that so-and-so?' we are satisfied.

Wax is a leveller. It prefers death to life. Good riddance, it says to the fearfully famous one as to the loved one, and now let's doll you up for your last party; to which sacred

17

and valedictory spree—democracy being what it is—we're all invited. Yet fame and top-lighting and the shadows cast a spell, and memory glides on through the halls where those who have sought power find—wax.

I'm relieved, I must say, not to come across too many friends. If wax wipes the grin off the politician, it robs virtue also. I shouldn't like to encounter here Van Gogh or Baudelaire, and there's not the least chance of doing so, or of surprising Beethoven and Goethe, Dostoevsky and Ibsen, Freud, Einstein, Sibelius. Shakespeare, it is true, attends, but he was a popular waxwork already, and here he is the mere acolyte of Sir James Barrie who sits— Literature in person—writing. A well-soaped vacuity seems the rule, and it makes Queen Elizabeth the First and Lloyd George akin. Only some duskiness of countenance or the wildest excess of face-hair can resist it.

As I wait in the vestibule I catch several people staring, looking away and then looking back, so that I find it necessary to give a little cough and flick another page. They move off discomfited, while my eye now strays to the second or infernal part of our entertainment, to reach which we must brave dungeons where the lost faces peer from grills and one pays a further ninepence.

Here lights and ceilings are low, stone walls sweat, gallows loom, unmentionable tortures are inflicted behind curtains, and visitors and visited at last mingle. Here are Smith and Robinson—no Jones, as yet. You and I walk on, but not Smith; his bath (here displayed) undid him. Baths, bread-knives, washing-lines, cups of tea or cocoa—these, horribly familiar, are instruments of power, as upstairs the signed document and the secret order. Do we celebrate bluff King Hal? Then let's not forget little Crippen, with only one wife put away, who starts forward in shabby,

ugly appeal: he would plead his case. They would all—
hideously—plead a case. This is where, in the thick of
Tussaudery, our sympathies and repulsions at last tighten,
and where also the art of the wax-modeller gains strength.

It has always surprised me that Madame Tussaud's,
which after all is one of our main repositories of popular
legend, should have grasped so uncertainly at its own
material. Where, for example, from along the road, is the

great Sherlock Holmes? His sitting-room (very carefully
worked out, by the way, a year or two ago) would surely
appeal, with that *second* waxwork in the window. Where
Johnson and Boswell, Fagin's den, the Loch Ness Monster,
Lady Macbeth sleep-walking, and King Alfred burning the
cakes? Shall Blondin disappear forever into that Niagara
over which he triumphantly rode?

'Well, so you've seen Mr. Christie,' said a fat owlish
man, coming up for air close by where I sat in the vesti-

bule, '*and* the string chair and the sink and the coal-scuttle———'

'I wonder,' interrupted his wife, a comfortable-looking woman, 'if the floorboards was real———'

There was an owlish child too, who was staring at me with a peculiar intensity of distrust.

'Don't touch!' cried his mother.

I started, or rather would have started had not something, the unholy enchantment of the place, prevented me.

The child trailed off, looking back from time to time at my immobility; and if at that instant, with loud cheerful cries, my friends hadn't shown up, I believe I should have gone on sitting there, one with the commissionaire on the landing and the policeman upstairs— one of *them*.

A Cry from the Underground

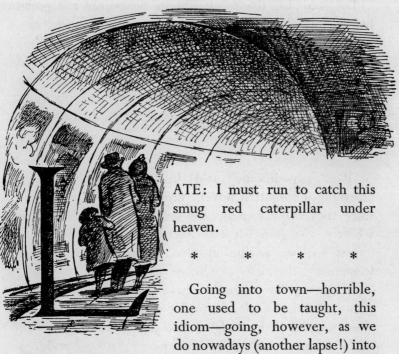

LATE: I must run to catch this smug red caterpillar under heaven.

*   *   *   *

Going into town—horrible, one used to be taught, this idiom—going, however, as we do nowadays (another lapse!) into town, neither on horse nor on foot, nor in spanking chaises, I bow scrupulously to the empty carriage. Forty-four seats invite me: what worlds divide the long public rows from the family (or perhaps kneeing) foursomes, and these again from the pews snug for two, stretchable for one—to say nothing of *strapontins* at the end! All mine!

Not for long, however. Others shove in, at first leisurely and then more and more like schoolboys kicked from behind. I settle for a pew where I can idle and read, and which at a later stage I shall defend strenuously against breathless women with bags and huge overcoated men.

*　　　*　　　*　　　*

The sunlight, the too-bright sunlight over the green belt, makes a last clutch at our knees; and we plunge.

Earthed!

Dark—but the dark becomes light, and a transformation is accomplished: in each one of us, secretly, swiftly, the individual is being tightly reined or loosed. We stare about us. We are—for the time being—Tube-folk, underground men.

*　　　*　　　*　　　*

'Tube expeditions,' said Julius Parkinghorn in a charming if forgotten novel, 'are the negation of travel, since they neglect means for ends; you can't even see where you're going; it is abstract travel.'

Just so: we voyage in idea, in intensity, in time. Remember, the cities of A.D. 2050 will be underground.

Of course, like others, we have our bus days when the crowds and the clouds, the prolonged stares into first-floor windows, the traffic dodgings and jams draw irresistibly; when we can almost agree (before jumping off and walking) that it is better to travel hopefully than to arrive.

Until recently we even had, should the rage take us, trams: those 'gondolas' of Victorian fancy, ting-tinging and pitching, rubbing sides, twinkling in the fogs they so loved. What is the trolley-bus but a bus that can't take the wrong turning?

*　　　*　　　*　　　*

The disposition of the long facing rows, the six-or-seven-a-sides, begins to make itself felt. Here will mingle public and performers. The masque will be tense. Not everyone may seem to be taking part, but those holding off will veil up with a newspaper, or close their eyes: acting for all they're worth. Much advertisement-reading with an overdone interest goes on in those seats too.

*　　*　　*　　*

Look, an old stager with a butterfly collar adjusting his spectacles to read the paper next door.

Others, by the way, always enjoy the best news. 'Nelson's Column Climbed' flashed at me across the carriage the other week, when all my poor sheet could manage was 'Peace Hopes Uncertain.'

*　　*　　*　　*

With the rush hour well past, half a dozen people are scattered about the public rows, waiting. Enter a young woman. Choosing rapidly, she places herself with a glass partition to this side and an empty seat, on which she establishes a handbag, to the other. Her legs are crossed to receive the notebook in which she begins—or rather, elaborately resumes—writing in pencil, with more pauses than words and an attention not of this world. Poetry, without a doubt. Yes, she has the finger tracery, the serious sunk eye, the shadow under the cheekbone, swan neck, and slope shoulders, all to match. And a little spring hat. But such a fine, alarmed, haunted, sweet-sad look! . . . She has taken the lead, and knows it.

Can that poem ever compare with the delightful business of writing it? One shouldn't ask; it's no concern of ours. Here the only talent is for being something or somebody—oneself, another, what matter? Perhaps that notebook, so displayed yet zealously guarded, contains no more than weak imitations of Keats. It might even be a shopping list.

*　　*　　*　　*

This little performance has the advantage, of course, of its setting: the top lighting, the hush in the tunnel and the flight of mildly lit stations, the sudden fish-like tangency of a passing train, could scarcely be improved on. And beyond, there's that larger drama requiring for its enactment halls, passage-ways, moving stairs. Mysterious gales wait at corners; trains seem to approach and then vanish away; telephone bells ring unanswerably. The crowd comes and goes. But always it leaves a residue, always on the platform there are a few who will wait for another train—and another. They will be found also wandering along remote connecting-ways or climbing forgotten spirals. They put pennies in old slot machines. One of them stands by a ventilation shaft, listening. They are trapped by the Inner Circle. After midnight their strange cries and stranger music—as we wait for a last train—echo underfoot, overhead. Who are they? Agoraphobes, tramps, lost souls (didn't Orpheus dare here for Eurydice?), middle-earthers, survivors of one war and early prospectors of the next. Tube folk; for whom our passage is a mere flittering of ghosts.

*　　*　　*　　*

At the moment, by the way, we are under Somers Town, that domain of the railway palace and the gasometer clump, before gaining (if it is a gain) Pentonville and the Angel.

24

The old chap with the butterfly collar, angrily with-drawing his attention, has cased his spectacles: either the news displeases him, or his neighbour has leant out of range.

Oh, I'd almost forgotten! 'From East Finchley to Morden (via the Bank) is a distance of seventeen and a quarter miles—the longest tunnel journey it is possible

to make on any railway in the world (the Simplon tunnel, next longest, is twelve and a quarter miles)'—Ward Lock's *Guide to London*, 1953.

*　　　*　　　*　　　*

There's no traveller in the world like the Londoner who spends anything from one-tenth to one-quarter of his day in going to and fro and about. Yet what is his dream? To travel, to 'get away.'

*　　　*　　　*　　　*

I shall never forget how, as a child, being dressed up for some occasion, I was perplexed by the old lady taking me,

25

who turned back at the tube entrance to remark 'Not today—I don't think I can face the drama of it: let's go by bus.' Strange words, whose meaning was hidden from me for a decade or more.

I grew up, so to speak, on the tube, went to school in it, sporting, unmistakably, a top-hat. Such, a time-honoured education required. It picked me out even in those days, the only toppers being those of a few city gentlemen or gentlemen on their way to funerals or Lord's. This was the old Hampstead and Highgate line (now at the heart of the Northern system), with carriages opening at the ends to swing gates and gate-men shouting the stations. What a clatter and what roaring gales through the tunnels! What strange smells from the dim red-and-white tiled platforms! How uncomfortable the shiny straw seats! My joy was to sit at the very back of the train and watch the bright circle of the station dwindle like a camera-lens stopped down.

But the 'drama of it' was beginning to grip me with curiosity and pleasure, and at moments almost with anguish.

* * * *

The delicate Poetess (I can't, you see, take my eyes off her) continues to play admirably. An old woman seated opposite glares, flashes her rings, blows cigarette smoke across; but not she or the murdered bird in her hair can distract for an instant from the work in progress.

Then a big man, hatless, with tie deranged, comes to sit a couple of seats away. He begins dabbing at one eye. At first we pay scant attention, being caught in a silken web, but then we note cotton wool, the head bowed forward, the uneasy shiftings and a curious helplessness in the hand

26

unemployed. Pain! This quite alters the situation. Furiously the old woman smokes and coughs: our swan, after some surreptitious glances, looks put out. What's this intrusion on sweet sorrow? A pain in the eye! Hardly decent! And how admirably now (and no doubt with good cause) he embodies it, so that we're uncomfortable and attentive to the further ends of the carriage. He dabs; she scribbles. She does her utmost, finding nobler words and gauging starrier distances; but it's no good. All eyes pass her by. And though this inconsiderately weeping lump gets out at the next station our thoughts follow him to hard hospital benches, tiled corridors, the desk and the instrument tray.

Then the question arises whether, a little later on (between Stockwell, say, and Clapham South) and upon audiences knowing nothing of the eye-sufferer, she can re-establish her spell. Not destiny, but destination, robs me of the answer: I must leap up in a panic and fly away through the doors as they snap at me.

*   *   *   *

I'm in time, and I've tasted Eternity.

The Room

T O the Reading Room—there's only one Reading Room—sooner or later we all go. We have texts to rifle, a genealogical tree to plant, a heresy to uproot. We start revolutions and mend socks. My own reason for going was to look up Thomson. Among the several James Thomsons mine was distinguished not as 'Poet' but as '(B.V.) Author of *The City of Dreadful Night*.' Thus already, in the catalogue, doubts were engendered. Was he, indeed, the poet he should be? Why wouldn't our pessimism look

28

at his? Would the luck never turn? 'Never!' The echo seemed to spring out of the floor, from Thomson himself. I looked round, but those on either side were busy attending to other voices: one, I thought (under cover of *The Free Negro in Virginia*), to Littlewood's.

Thomson, however, who never fails to mitigate for me the approaching joys of Christmas, was less my concern at the moment than the room I was sitting in, that Rotunda from which, off and on, we had been banished, almost a decade, to rectilinear exile on the north side. One needs the great O; on each and all should rise, like Shakespeare's brow, its bright dome. Roundheads we may become, square never. And, without thinking, I, an infrequent visitor, had marched up between the Ionic pillars, through the revolving door, and straight across to the old narrow conduit. There were Julius Caesar and Nero, Panizzi over the door. There it was, open and, at 11.45 in the morning, surprisingly vacant. I took a deep breath; the fog seemed to have cleared. New paint and furnishings were in place —blue-grey, cream, and gilt. Dawn after dusk! It took, as I chose my seat, some little getting used to. But the long desks still radiated from an official hub; two galleries circled inaccessible shelves; higher and higher the eye soared over acres of cream paint to fix at length on the dome, through which a winter sun, brightly diffused, brought eternity to bear on those settled and settling below. It was the old Reading Room, though in a new edition.

Then, just under the dome, my eye caught a difference. The names, the names were gone! There were, you remember, nineteen of these below nineteen windows— a twentieth being occupied by the clock—beginning Chaucer, Caxton, Tindale . . . and ending, I think, with

Tennyson and Browning. Now there are nineteen gilt panels. Will the names come back? Or some of them, but not others? Macaulay—have they found him a corner in the lumber room, from which delightedly, in 1982, some Philadelphian will exhume him? Are there voting lists, canvassings, secret ballots? Might we—the readers and ticket-holders—join in? Oughtn't *The Times* correspondence to know?

It takes longer than I had remembered for the books ordered to be received, and I wander off to stretch my legs through the museum; among winged lions, bulls; pre-dynastic man in his sarcophagus, an agony perpetuated in more than parchment, with the knees drawn up and the hand warding off—French schoolgirls, pastors from the Netherlands throw a startled, serious glance; the Elgin rooms, empty as heaven, in which rise a terrified horse's head, headless women running, unsexed warriors; and so to the battle with centaurs, not quite decided by Time. There is no nightmare to equal that of mythology.

Somewhat reduced I find my way back to G5, where a small pile of books awaits me. I press the button over the desk wall facing me; strip lighting (new indeed!) lights up for me during the next few hours lugubrious shadows. My American biography improves on Salt, substituting also linen covers for cardboard, and to hand there are the translations from Leopardi (which I've yet to read), the usual perceptive Frenchman, a psychiatrist who knows everything. The quotations lure me on, Matilda flares, day (overhead as on the page) turns to night, all will end in drink—poor Thomson, whose failing as a poet is that he is too sober.

Here, of course, he worked and occupied, not far off in Huntly Street, the last of a succession of single rooms.

Now why not *his* name for a window? Why not, for a change, Great Readers? Gibbon, Burke, Lamb, Dickens, Carlyle (who complained of having to sit on the top of a ladder), Marx the unreadable, starving Gissing, smug Thackeray: they would at least have the claim of having stared at the spaces they fill. First, without question, would come Butler and Miss Savage—joined in one panel? —whose delightfully acrid courtship over ten years had the Reading Room for its trysting-place.

The bell rings for 5 (in Butler's day it was 7); Thomson, sadly near the end, is left adrift in rags; Littlewood's and *The Free Negro in Virginia* are packed up; and out I walk, with the occupational cold bum and shrugged shoulders, into the mauveness of a dusk in which a barrel-organ apologetically drops padded notes.

The Romantic life, it sometimes seems to me, is not the poet's, the airman's, the spy's, or the lover's, but the incorrigible student's. Addiction to print is an intoxication compared with which opium or alcohol offers the mildest temptations. With what greed, what lust, will they, these word-swallowers and chain-readers, fling themselves upon a new arrival of books, explore and enjoy them, ravish them, disembowel them, and then in a serious brisk manner walk off to order more! What lunch to compare with the poached egg sandwiched between chapters of the *Decline and Fall*, the cigarette on the steps, smoked (as a cigarette should be smoked) pacing up and down, with an eye for a November sun, a trifle of mist, and pigeons flying across the forecourt?

A day at the museum has revived in me longings for dissipation, but in the gait and faces of those walking away I see, not without envy, that the day itself should be the dissipation, to be followed by cold supper and bed.

31

The Enchanted Park

CHIMBORAZO, Cotopaxi, avers the poet, had stolen his heart away. In my case it was Hyde Park. Peering out from a bus through the snow, I saw a gentleman on one of the park seats reading a newspaper. Look, I cried, look! Hyde Park, observed my father; and that explained it.

Especially as, in later years, I was warned against ever going there. Black railings protected me against the crocus and litter-strewn grass, swans' wings, tramps, horses, occasional gunfire or band music, the bowler-hatted stranger with a sweet tooth. Dogs went mad, boys drank deep of infected fountains, and cricket wasn't cricket—in Hyde Park. Somewhere even lurked Mr. Hyde. Several of my friends used to go there, and I knew them as damned irretrievably.

And when at last I did venture in, nothing more happened than that I tripped over a rail and was helped up by someone introducing himself as the King of Bohemia.

The charm still persists. I like to spend the day there, preferably a day when there's so much to do that one decides to do nothing. I'll lie in the grass, watch the clouds, listen to the traffic mutter. Something will turn up, if it's only sheep: such grimy sheep as haunt a West Riding moor. There will, mysteriously, be classical dancers in a dell. Policemen will shoot off on bicycles. Over a fisherman's shoulder I'll gaze into Serpentine waters (what woman would understand this?), join the talking groves at Marble Arch, walk anywhere.

Bewildering is the choice of things one can do—or others can. Ride, run, row, swim, play bowls, watch the cars go by, read Grodzinsky or Mrs. Christie, peel one's socks off, contemplate the Albert Memorial (has it never been climbed?), take flowers to the dogs' cemetery or tar and feathers to Physical Energy, hold a jet-plane on a leash, loose a balloon, fly a kite, launch one's fancy on that Round Pond where once Shelley, sailing paper-boats, was seen plain.

In Hyde Park I include (as some may not) Kensington Gardens: all part of that stretch of country between Notting Hill and Whitehall traversed, morning and evening, by high officials walking to and from their high places. One of their ukases has recently torn down the elms along the Broad Walk, as though a freak storm had passed; and hundreds more may follow; if not, we're told, they will

B

fall on us. However, these victims of elm disease or departmental fury will by their very absence continue to engross us. Hyde Park is much haunted. The Crystal Palace, that metropolitan fairy tale, glitters afar, with the incident of its opening when, in the middle of the 'Hallelujah Chorus,' a gorgeous Chinaman prostrated himself before the Queen. Room was quickly found for him between the Archbishop of Canterbury and the Duke of Wellington, and so the procession moved off. Too late it was discovered that this Eastern luminary owned a junk on the Thames doing a brisk trade with visitors at a shilling a head.

There's a tug honking now. Perhaps I've imagined it. My thoughts seem to come back to boats (was it George III who staged a vast mimic battle on the Serpentine?), and my steps to the Round Pond. This regatta will last the whole summer, with gala days over week-ends.

Everything that floats has a place, from match-boxes to the tall yacht that brushes aside battleships. A paddle-steamer encounters an up-ended duck. Motor-boats whirr by clippers and, suddenly quiet, re-enact the fable of tortoise and hare. Except on afternoons when not a ripple stirs and discomfited owners waggle sticks or throw pebbles, these are still days of sail.

Then the sensation: a drone like a may-bug's, patter of feet, cries and coos, and there, where interest points, is the latest speed-boat performing prodigies. Not only, half out of water, can it make rings round every other craft there: it does, it makes rings. It sees ducks, and flies straight at them. It circles a swan, round and round, and that monumental bird is made a goose, like Falstaff in the forest.

From an excited urchin I pick up the magic words

'radio-controlled speedboat,' and by pushing in I discover
two pipe-smoking dons (so they seem) with a couple of
boxes and a hand-dial. They surpass themselves in figures
of eight, without a smile. But the faces round are worth
watching. Some future Jutland or River Plate is being
decided.

The solemn tweedy pair are young compared with
others enjoying themselves in earlier ways. One frail old
man acquires a demonic energy in deftly turning his ship
when it threatens to land; then, angrily scattering children
and infants, he runs off at top speed to meet his pride on
the opposite shore.

There are, a little way off, quieter old men flying kites.

I know very well where this leads. On some distant
birthday you will find *me* here; but in which rank—boatman or kite-man—time and eccentricity alone can decide.

Horse Show

YESTERDAY in London, among the many convergences that unknown to us swell our traffic block, one could not fail to declare itself. Sixty-seven costermongers, some in pearlies, with new-varnished carts, had a date. Ponies jingled and mokes tripped it. From Bermondsey and Battersea, Wandsworth and Deptford they came; and 6 p.m. at the White City saw the first of them enter the arena. There all the week, in an International Horse Show, aristocrats of their world had been stepping, rearing, cavorting, jumping, galloping, trotting; the Costers' Turnout brought, I won't say a touch of nature, but common kind. There were sympathetic claps from the public benches. The stadium for this occasion, when it is barely a tenth filled, divides neatly into two: nobs on the one side, plebs on the other. Even the horses seem to recognize this. They kowtow there, play up here. They know their place, a rather exalted one. Whatever you may say about the horse in these oil-driven days, he remains (given the opportunity) a gentleman. No dog can boast that, and many a dog has tried.

The afternoon had started with jumping. A course of a dozen obstacles, artfully crisscrossed, simulated a run with hedges, five-bar gates, fences, walls, higher or lower, but all with dislodgable parts: some took them almost walking, others preferred a bold dash, though speed and style here counted for nothing. One got to know the hazards, if not the chances; often the more spirited kind would sail through a blissful first half, to pull up amazed before the painted brick wall that barred a way to the second. The winner of this competition was none other than Foxhunter, though on the Wednesday afternoon we missed seeing him in action. He led the parade: a great sportsman! The band played 'Voices of Spring.' On either side of me cock-a-hoop sat men with small caps and big moustaches. 'Jereboams!' said one. 'That'll teach the damned Russians,' said the other.

Then there was a judging of hunters, seen in three actions, walking, cantering, galloping, as dictated by a little bowlegged man in gold-braided scarlet with his mouth to a long horn; streaming across the field they let go, though fashion no longer allows coat-tails to fly with horses'. Trotting, the most perverse of fancies, followed:

37

these ponies seem too diminutive for their masters, and tight-reining has induced a style as archly stepping, and to some delectable, as the Hippodrome chorus. The counties were brought back by the arrival, or flooding, of the Pytchley Hounds, which like well-ordered quicksilver spilt round flower beds and judges' stands. With nothing in view, except perhaps a delayed breakfast, they kept up the liveliest pretence of September mornings, foxes in plenty. Hunting in 1952, the programme assured us, holds its own. Golden days may be over, but—despite shut gates and scent-destroying manures—a silver age is still ours. The fox remains delicately poised between extinction and preservation, now harried, now encouraged. 'D'ye ken John Peel?' inquired the band bluffly; and how could anyone argue with that?

The afternoon, till then cool and grey, broke into bright, dappled, lolloping clouds, so that to match them, one looked for a buxom shire horse or shiny brewer's pride. But this wasn't their occasion. Elegance and metal held sway. What could have been more eye-taking than the four black chargers of the Household Cavalry, alert for tent-pegging? For a moment they brought back glory, when a horse with ideals could be shot from under a general. Even today (how many income-tax sufferers know this?) a gentleman riding to and from his office may claim five pounds relief. The dark lancers swept by the royal enclosure; four lances aimed, stabbed; three met the ground, and only one was lifted in triumph. Style, even in tent-pegging, isn't everything. This particular prize was carried off with almost grim efficiency by the Lancashire Police.

More jumping, this time with speed as a main factor; and a dashing Irish captain—fit hero for a Dornford Yates

novel—surpassed everything with the gay faultless round
so many riders must dream of. I had grown rather dreamy
myself. Sensations were over; another roundabout of
trotting was due, then the costers; it was growing colder,
with threats of rain. When would the bars open, and what
were my neighbours bandying across me? 'Union Jack
Stakes every time!' insisted one. 'Give me the Tally-Ho
Stakes!' replied the other; and then, deferring to me,
'What do you say?'

I'm afraid I said, without thinking, 'Soho steaks.'

They were puzzled for a second during which the
enormity of my lapse came home to me.

'So-ho! so-ho!' I hurried on, trying to make the best
of it.

The band struck up something out of the *Mikado*, and
the first of the high-stepping ponies—over fourteen hands,
I noted with desperate interest—were away; but silence
gripped the three of us sitting there on our bench. A
single accusation shone out from the red faces on either
side of me. *Cannibal!*

Not a word was spoken. I left as soon as I decently
could; and it will be many years before I poke myself into
a horse show again. Outside the White City lorries were
plunging and cars swerving, creatures of the new world.
One poor old blinkered nag stood in dejection, with no
thought outside a dropped nosebag.

Kisses Before Noon

I AM a film critic, differing in this from the book critic, who should be able to read, and again from the dramatic critic, who must remember Shakespeare and Hazlitt, and suit himself to that witching hour when taxis flit to catch rising curtains.

Not so the film critic. No mere trappings of glamour—opera-cloak or glasses, sad-glad whiskies at the bar, critical attitudes—will satisfy him: Glamour itself is his date, at 10.30 a.m.

Already at Clapham South, as I mount bus stairs, my

high destiny picks me out from others. While they may splutter and cough, curse the weather, scan prices and futures, smoke or joke nervously, I am to meet Miss Dietrich on the ranch. They won't be meeting Miss Dietrich till Friday at the very earliest; and it's now, of course, Monday morning.

Fog curls round a lamp-post, and all about me, as the bus plunges or creeps forward, are such evidences of human futility as painters on ladders, nonagenarians filling in forms in post-offices, butchers waving sausages, gas-men rising out of manholes, lorries backing into impossible archways, dogs running off on errands, trains screaming, and tall chimneys manufacturing sulphur clouds. All are exerting themselves—how pathetically!—to deny what it is that makes the world go round. With my orange-and-white card marked 'Back Circle,' I know better.

I am elate, vicious, as might be one who has laced his cereal with gin, or expects to be in Cairo by lunch-time. The wretched work-conscious looks which I seem to share with my fellow-passengers are a blind. At heart I am treasonable, a fellow-traveller in the cause of pleasure.

We charge through streets where everyone subscribes to some useful occupation such as giving short weight for potatoes or digging up the pavement. An undertaker surveys through the gilt lettering of his window a pedestrian crossing.

And it's Love, Love, Love that makes the world go round!

The West End brings at last a whiff of reality, though even here window-cleaners tend to clean windows and typists to tickle keys. But traffic halts; time ceases to count. Our bus-driver, softly bumping the bus ahead, leans out to engage the irresistible conductress so approached.

Tickets are torn up. We gladly get off and walk. The sun shines. There is music in doorways. Bubbles float through the air to cling to an elderly nose or disappear into upstairs windows.

Evening papers open out like daisies. Bootblacks polish a philosophy. Those who have been born a couple of ice-cream parfaits below par are catching up. The glossy shop-windows offer furs, rainbows, jewels, macaroons, levitations of hats, live poodles, bread-fruit, saloon cars, tropical sunsets, and oneself in ghostly possession of all.

Hail, Piccadilly! Leicester Square! To that monarch of pleasure-lovers, Shakespeare, is dedicated the garden where under the trees sit lovers, tramps, schoolgirls, soldiers, duchesses, messenger boys folding their messages into darts. Old age bowls its hoops and great-grand-children get their milk teeth into Ovid. Under a bench is the shoe from which last night's champagne was drunk. The Bard himself loafs eternally, reclining one arm on his works and extending the other in a courtly do-as-you-please gesture. The hand is missing, lost presumably during the Blitz; but that's neither here nor there to a playwright who has suffered worse cuts. He gazes, with that silly-willy look of his, at the portals of one cinema, and there are cinemas all round: this is the very heart of Filmlandia. My invitation takes me to that Versailles or Xanadu upon which cling men with letters big as themselves, as they take down one stupendous billing to replace it by another.

The press show is due to begin. I cross over, exchange hard pavement for deep red carpet, and sunlight for chandelier, proffer my invitation card to the Ruritanian door-girl who will take half, intercept a host's smile meant, I think, for the gentleman behind who is already muttering

'A longshoreman's picture, tear-provoking, rib-splitting, spiritual, lustful, great,' and hurry to take my seat among the thousands waiting.

You would wonder that there could be so many film critics in existence. But here from all parts of the world we flock to every first morning. Our enthusiasm knows no limits: the ballet fan, by comparison, is a sick chick. No film ever goes by us unclapped. We are astounded. We are assaulted, ravished. Our only defence against this orgy, which takes us three or four times a week, year in and year out, is that craft which for the sake of immediacy we pursue *in situ*, scribbling by the light of pocket torches. Thence, from that glow-worm rustling at the quick of cinema, issue the epithets and encomiums that must make us bless the tongue that Amanda Ros used.

But already stage lights are dimming, music stuns with its first catastrophe, curtains divide, the hairdresser has helped and the censor allows. She who is everyone's temptation will soon be ours. Where are my torch and my notebook? My lips, parted . . . ?

A Touch of the Sun

'I AM told——' began the informed voice; but at that moment the 'Z' bus arrived, and we in the queue-pen, leaving Wimbledon, moved up. Still dazzled by sun and tennis we were trying to get used to a world in which we weren't all begging bears, swivelling the head from right to left, left to right.

It is a strange sensation, when you haven't encountered it for a few years, this hypnotism of tennis. Brought up as a cricketer, I take a naturally lazy view of games: elegance and distance, the pause, the Pateresque devotion to style, the strolling in, out, and about, time counted in hours, in days, in intervals during which the play may be criticized and forgotten—these I tend to assume when I or others go into white. Tennis, from this point of view, is shocking. It is hemmed in, man to man or woman to woman; it can't take walks, it labours the point; the clash of dissimilars is brought down to an endless variation of if-then and either-or: in fact, not a drama but a dialogue. Terse, thrilling, gloriously certain, and (dare I venture?) a shade monotonous. No *deus ex machina* will ever, nimbly or portentously, order his crane to be lowered. Unless weatherwise. On that afternoon the centre court's

44

tarpaulins were tight-rolled. But would the succession of fine days hold?

Like heat-waves, champions fade quickly. Here is yet another game which we English have sent bumbling into the void, to welcome back jet-engined. The ingenious Major Wingfield who in 1874 patented his 'new and improved portable court' and three years later succeeded in adding Lawn Tennis to the other attractions of the Wimbledon Croquet Club, ought to be statued at the main entrance with his hat off. It is an affair now between Americans and the others. If the others—not often ourselves—snatch a point or a promotion, we feel rarely bucked. What still is most ours is the green grass, the cries of 'love' and 'deuce,' the rather devastating correctitude that has taken the place of gentlemanliness. Mannerisms (what time is there for them?) have been ironed out; mood, in the close-up, is so curbed that if today a player were to fling down his racquet, all Wimbledon would go up to a twang of snapped strings.

The crowd is almost too well-behaved to be true. It (or the gallery part of it) queues all night, stands all day in the sun, applauds with mild handclaps, has learnt no vocabulary of encouragement or abuse. Should some visitor—from Neptune, presumably—after inquiring what tennis is all about, settle himself to forty winks (as apparently did at least one gentleman the other week), there will be damaging letters in the Press. One such letter, which I had read on my way to Wimbledon, had determined me at all costs to keep my mouth shut and my eyes open. But as the afternoon wore on with a succession of adroit, tense, perfectly conducted duels, and the hot sun crept up from my knees to my chin, I couldn't help *thinking*—while, I hope, outwardly doing my bit as a

45

tennis-watcher—of pelota matches in San Sebastian. A hard angry echoing game, neither so varied nor so agreeably stylish as tennis: muscular, dramatic, exclusively male. Particularly the bookies haunted me. There they would stand in a row looking up at the boxes and galleries that line one side of the court, miming, cajoling, singing out odds, adeptly flinging and catching the little wooden ball in which a bet is contained. Sometimes, when the rallies were ding-dong, the market chorus would die away, sometimes it would reach a crescendo inciting to both spectators and players; more and more furious would grow the harsh clack of wood against stone, the rivalry of odds . . .

The Wimbledon sun had reached my nose-tip. In one court (a gentle ripple of applause reaching us over the mound) the crowd has been rebuked for too vigorously supporting Little Mo; one strangled cry of 'Budge!' had lent feeling to the untheatrical decline of Patty; we hadn't bawled, we hadn't betted, we hadn't waved or leapt to our feet (except for the arrival of the Duchess of Kent); we had sat back on uncomfortable seats, or fainted—two hundred of us—to be carried away.

And now, for the day at least, it is all over.

'I am told—' repeats the informed voice—the odour of hay and petrol is strong as smelling salts, and across the way, amazingly, two old men are ambling at golf by a lake —golf!—'I am told that the Queen is making some new Knights of the Thistle; who are they?'

Who indeed? Already the spell has been broken; we are beginning to come out of our trance of loves and deuces, vantage here, vantage there, Seixas, Little Mo, Ip and Tsai. There is the sun, that huge bright ball, motionless, fairly asking for it; but, as the bus jogs along, we feel after our pennies, with no more thoughts for a volleyer.

46

IT begins in the horse-butcher's, where nobody ventures except on his dog's account.

So I open with 'Find me a high bit, I'm off fishing.'

'My uncles,' remarks the butcher, a dainty man— 'my uncles go fishing.'

'Do you go with them?'

'Me? Not likely.'

And he recedes through the doorway into that tiled chamber from which automatically one averts the eye.

*   *   *   *

Really it began long before, with our friends who took a Frenchman walking. It was a fine day and the scenery pleasant, but no Frenchman just walks in the country, and soon this one was plucking edible snails from a

47

hillside. After lunch they came to a valley with a little stream. 'Crayfish!' he exclaimed, flung himself full-length, slid his arm into the water, and brought up two of them.

That set it off. He showed them how to construct nets, how to weight and bait them, how to catch your crayfish and cook him. Several expeditions had been made, and this year we had been admitted to the secret.

Not that the local people would look at crayfish, or the owner of the right bank, a retired military man; but should any restaurant keeper or Soho provisioner get to hear, that would be the end of our crayfish. Already, you see, ours.

*   *   *   *

'Where'd you say you were going?' asks the butcher, with his head in the safe.

'Oh,' I reply, 'it's just outside'—and pull myself up. Men who would arrive after dark and fling in, if you please, a horse's head (so the Frenchman had averred), all nested with twigs, and next day haul it out with every crayfish adhering. The uncles!

'—Miles away,' I conclude; 'that's the bother.'

'Just wondered,' says he, hacking.

*   *   *   *

It's a fortnight since we made our first foray. Dull weather. The crayfish is nocturnal. But some fishermen favour a come-and-go sunlight, and one relates how, on a hot afternoon, having stretched himself on the bank to read, he heard a strange scratching noise and looked up to see them ascending out of the water in hundreds, in thousands . . .

The valley seemed to encourage secrecy—this or the

next? Our road narrowed and then with the twists and descents of a well-kept lane we were in the village; a couple of score old houses, two pubs, a church, and the stream. This, winding, we followed down, past boys with jam jars and nets, girls on stiles, to the semi-privacy of the fields. Stumpy willows; cattle bridge, and no cattle; behind us the village roofs, ahead ploughed acres. For a half-mile or so it was all ours—and the crayfish's.

* * * *

'How's that?' asks the butcher, returning.
Horrible!—just the thing!

* * * *

We had settled on a convenient bend where there was a bedding of water-thyme and the current ran deep, and lowered our nets—noisomely baited—at six-foot intervals. Ten minutes to wait.

But it was such a little, such an ordinary stream, and not a crayfish in sight.

Grass-heads swayed. A faint squealing as of pigs came from a mechanical rake on the hill. The wooded ridges hedged us in from who knows what tentacles of suburb, what roaring roads.

A train nosed up the valley, 'Nice train,' said one. 'In seventy years,' said another, 'someone will be saying "nice jet."' 'Perhaps he'll be crayfishing.' 'Let's pull up.' It wasn't time, but we rushed, each to a net, and lifted . . .

* * * *

'Crayfish,' says the butcher, sniffing; 'can't say I fancy 'em myself.'

* * * *

49

Two came up with the first net, five with the second, several more with the third and fourth. Soon we were snatching them out—mud-coloured, clinging, clawing, hissing things—in half-dozens and dozens, to be crammed into a straw shopping bag strung along the top with a gap. Some fell, backing quickly into hummocks; others waved wicked pincers, or rattled that tail-piece grandly known as the 'telson.' Within the hour, bag full, we were in one of the pubs discussing with the landlord everything except crayfish.

We took away a big bottle of cider. Having caught your crayfish, you keep him twenty-four hours (so that he'll clear), and then cook and eat him: a sequence of mingled alarms and delights.

In the night I woke to hear a stirring and crackling as of newly lit twigs. The crayfish, still sewn up tight, in the bath.

Then the next evening, dreading what was to happen, with the crayfish suddenly let loose in the bath like giant ants discovered, and a dixie bubbling with cider and water, onion, herbs . . . I won't go on. It wasn't quite as bad as we'd feared, and with the first mouthfuls we forgave one another.

*   *   *   *

My conversation with the butcher has now reached double tracks.

'That ought to make them bite,' I agree, recoiling; but then advancing, '*How's the fillet?*'

'I'll wrap it up well. *Very nice and tender.*'

'Good. *Don't wrap them up together.*'

'*Two and ninepence do you?*'

'All right. *Which is which?* Thank you, good day.'

'Good fishing.'

*   *   *   *

That steak was the best I'd tasted in months, and we had a bumper catch.

One thing, don't let your crayfish catch you. He may stray, disconcertingly, in railway trains or, worse, in your own house. Once let him peep at you round the coal-scuttle or from a cushion, and you're lost. I know a poor fellow who, starting as we did, now has a crayfish in a tank on his window-sill. He feeds it with garden worms; he watches over its moults, and receives its sometimes painful caresses.

The Pleasures of Whitaker

MONG calendars big and small, some that tear off and some that click on, some with a little red window and others (now rare) revolved by the clock, nature-loving calendars and Shakespeare calendars and calendars given to nuts and wine, or nuts and bolts—among all, or rather apart from them, stands *Whitaker*.

Events and people are his love, festivals, law terms, battles, licences, royalty—but especially people. Few are the mornings, however dark, without their influence. They rise and shine, even if we don't. 'Get born,' they seem to be saying, if they say anything—'do as we've done, die, and perhaps one day you'll find yourself in *Whitaker*.'

His year—which is ours also—opens quietly.

1. 𝕮𝖎𝖗𝖈𝖚𝖒𝖈𝖎𝖘𝖎𝖔𝖓. 𝟭𝖘𝖙 𝕾𝖚𝖓. 𝖆𝖋𝖙𝖊𝖗 𝕮𝖍𝖗𝖎𝖘𝖙𝖒𝖆𝖘. NEW YEAR'S DAY.
2. General James Wolfe born, 1727.
3. C. R. Attlee born, 1883. J. E. Flecker died, 1915.
4. Sir Isaac Pitman (Shorthand) born, 1813.
5. Sir Humbert Wolfe born, 1885.
6. 𝕰𝖕𝖎𝖕𝖍𝖆𝖓𝖞. Twelfth Day. Fanny Burney died, 1840.

So far, if great moments have been few, there has been gentle insistence. We are more swayed than we think. Did Johnson's 'little Fanny' really see 1840, and was Sir Isaac, with his new hieroglyphics, in time to provoke her? Or take Wednesday with its thought, 'Today was born Mr. Attlee.' At once we reach for our least obtrusive suit; a keenness without zest guides our shaving; we are spry, dull, decent—until Flecker arrives. Too late now to change prose for verse, pin-stripe for, say, plum corduroy, but we manage to bundle a gorgeously coloured handkerchief into the cuff. Whitehall! Yasmin!

Except for storms on the 22nd (Byron and Strindberg born), January is mild, with one day such as only *Whitaker* brings:

8.   Plow Monday. Ada Rehan died, 1916.

What kind of a Monday is that? And who's she? One can't know both, yet see how two hemispheres are brought together. Instinct—and *Whitaker's* art—make it certain that the lady belongs to musical comedy; gone, alas, but on Plow Monday, returning. The month ends with (on the 27th), a most exquisite conjunction of Mozart born and Verdi dead.

Still under their influence, perhaps, February plumps in with:

Dame Clara Butt born.

All those weeks are memorable:

Feb. 1.   Dame Clara Butt born.
  2.   𝔓urification. Candlemas. James Joyce born.
  9.   Darnley died.
 10.   Queen Victoria married.
 16.   Ember Day. Li Hung Chang born.
 19.   Maurus Jokai born.

Far breezes, strange influences are stirring. March brings gales, quickly subsided.

Mar. 14.   'Timeless' Test Match abandoned, 1939.

15.   German troops occupied Prague, 1939.

16.   W. M. Surtees (Jorrocks) died, 1864.

Gloriously uncertain is April:

Apr. 6.   Danton died. Victor Gollancz born,
and

20.   A. Hitler, born 1889. (Summer Time begins 2 a.m., 21st)

but to close with the tender regrets of

28.   Nellie Farren died, 1904

—footlights again, of course.

Then May is the fair, fresh time one might expect, though there's no mistaking the nip in the air on the 27th:

John Calvin died, 1564. Mrs. Bloomer born, 1818.

More than time separates them, yet they are one.

Through the high summer of June–July one loses count of the hours and days, so that not even *Whitaker* can distinguish them.

August brings rains, and from the brimming butts and flooded pitches comes, on the 20th, 'Mosquito Day (1897). Gino Watkins died, 1932.'

But September—what cataclysms, what catastrophes!—reassurance must be far sought:

Sept. 1.   **15th 𝔖un. after 𝔗rin.** Germany invaded Poland, 1939.

2.   Fire of London, 1666. G. R. Sims born, 1847.

3.   Gt. Britain and France at war with Germany, 1939.

4.   French Republic proclaimed, 1870.

5.   Malta captured, 1800. Victorien Sardou born, 1831.

6.　The Marne, 1914. Sir Walford Davies born, 1869.

7.　Thomas Coutts (Banker) born, 1735.

October might pass us by but for a single day which is pure *Whitaker*:

Oct. 7.　Bidassoa, 1813. Sir Henry Taschereau born, 1836.

The autumn seems favourable to pairing days. We have Madame de Maintenon and Sir William Orpen together, and Picasso and W. G. Grace. Neither perhaps quite achieves the thrilling consonance of Agincourt and Balaclava, but there's a felicity in

J. B. Hobbs born, 1882. Noël Coward born, 1899.

Here a problem arises. The two exactly fill their line; not a word, not a letter may be added. With J. B. Hobbs now Sir Jack Hobbs, what will happen to Mr. Coward?

Whitaker teaches us that if people, well-known people, are born, they also die. There are vacancies—two splendid ones, on June 15 with 'Magna Carta Sealed' and on Oct. 30 with 'Joanna Southcott died'; though some might prefer to share with Samuel Smiles or Freud.

The year ends nobly. To the blustering ring of

Dec. 26. St. Stephen. Boxing Day. Dog Muzzling
　　　　Order, 1890

—a most expressive line—there succeeds the elegiac beauty of

Dec. 31. Skating on Thames at Windsor, 1890

than which no poet could have devised a more fitting conclusion.

Like many highly allusive works it can boast far more pages of annotation than text, as apparent right ascension and declension of planets, high and low tides, phases of the moon, civil and nautical twilights, and what not else of Zodiacal and commercial interest. There are such footnotes as 'Turkish National Holiday,' 'Borough Councillors to be Nominated' and the pure lilt of 'Dividends Due': rejected lines which might well have graced the text.

My copy is dated 1940. Whether more recent editions improve or not on this text I don't know, but it has grown so familiar I couldn't bear one word altered. I cherish also his **𝔓𝔯𝔦𝔫𝔠𝔦𝔭𝔞𝔩 𝔅𝔯𝔦𝔱𝔦𝔰𝔥 𝔞𝔫𝔡 𝔍𝔯𝔦𝔰𝔥 𝔖𝔬𝔠𝔦𝔢𝔱𝔦𝔢𝔰 𝔞𝔫𝔡 𝔍𝔫𝔰𝔱𝔦𝔱𝔲𝔱𝔦𝔬𝔫𝔰** in a lighter vein.

These are pure pleasure. *Whitaker* has his uses, no doubt, too, on Precedence or the American gallon.

Cat and Dog

T has been raining cats and dogs. Don't we, living or working in London, take too many things, too many people for granted? I found myself the other day sidling Vincent Square, that green acreage where they still play football, and more than one game of football, with the glum terraces looking on; and I might have been taking a short cut from Victoria to Westminster, or aiming to get into the Army and Navy Stores by the back way. In fact I was making for an entrance on the other side of the square.

The door opened, I stepped into the presence of two hundred cats. Not, of course, thronging: a crowd of cats is no more thinkable than a crowd of cat-burglars or cuckoos. These were on show, each situated in a wire compartment, and the compartments set side by side to form rows or streets along which humanity shuffled.

As I had never been to a cat show before—this was the Southern Counties Championship All Breed Show at the Royal Horticultural Hall—it took me some little time to get used to the arrangements. Simply to walk round wasn't at all easy. Everyone seemed to be up to something. Bottles and hot-water bottles were being fetched to and fro; hands dived into cages to readjust blankets; tough-looking exhibitors were swapping information, prices, and gossip ('Yes, Miss Horroway-Jones, we know *you* bred them, but who was the father?'); an old gentleman with his walking-stick rattled along the wire roofs to make 'em look up, showing mild eyes of topaz or beryl; there were visitors with notebooks and a few waiting with pussy faces or noises for a cat to talk to; and from time to time white-coated judges, of whom there seemed to be legions, would pounce, seize an animal, weigh it up and smack it down, pull its tail, and explore it unmercifully, though at arms' length. On the fringe sat a little quiet man smoking a pipe and offering for sale the *Tailwagger*; and boxes rattled for kind causes.

The objects of these attentions were incomparably at ease. They sat or coiled, basked, blinked, and snoozed, in a silence, a contemplation that was absolute. And what beauties! White Manx, tortoiseshell, marmalade (the only marmalade), Siamese mushroom-brown and smoke-blue, chocolate-box huggables, big organge-eyed madams in furs, quick-stepping Abyssinians, chinchilla, Burmese. I don't know which I admired most: perhaps the Abyssinians and the Burmese—they burn bright.

For a couple of days I couldn't wriggle out of their influence (do the élite of the Southern Counties also adorn fences and gaze out from the forests of the night under stationary vans?); and then came Cruft's. This name with the shaggy-waggy or skinny-winny appeal rises up every year to summon our bull-dog breed. What, not been to Cruft's? That had indeed been my lamentable state till the other afternoon, when I called in at Olympia.

Let's suppose (absurdly, of course) that you've never seen Cruft's. For the occasion all Olympia has been set out with rings in which the various classes are being judged. Each ring, as a matter of fact, is a square surrounded by seats. There you may settle, enjoying the terrier trot and sharing the flutter of the exhibitor who, brush in hand, will add the final touch to his dog's moustache, make his tail curve higher. Judging is meticulous; and after a while you may tire of seeing how master and dog should go for a run. So you exchange Norwich terriers for Afghan wolfhounds—quite another story. Or stroll between the rings to a periphery where, in clumps, all those dogs not immediately under a judge's eye wait their turn in cubicles. Among Basenjis and Salukis, bloodhounds, deerhounds, and elkhounds, Rhodesian Ridgebacks and Finnish Spitz, you may well get carried away into a region from which there is no return. The grave welcome from some is no less compelling than the nerves, the operatic nerves, of others.

However, tear yourself away in the end you must, if only to do the balcony, which has its own charm of toy dogs and a view over the whole concourse. Here, as on some exotic sea-front, you encounter silks and scents and poms, furs leading furs, Papillons wistful and pretty in a ring. Don't miss, side by side in pagodas, the twin Pekes! Mind that Chihuahua! And should this promenade prove a little too dainty, there's always the balcony rail to lean on, and the crowds, the rings, the baying and stewarding below.

Dogs! What—one may wonder, before this amazing disparity—*is* a dog? The gnat Chihuahua and the bloodhound of melancholic aspect seem hardly to speak the same language. Yet theirs is a world in common, struggling with success and failure, big business or little, sport, leisure, ideals. They look up, having an ancestry, a past, to live down. They verge upon tragedy. Dog is underdog. Who can meet his eye—that alert eye of sentiment—without gushing or domineering?

And cats? Their eyes marvellously they let shine, they prowl and spring and laze, and about them there's a something peaky and antic one doesn't hesitate to make fun of.

To make fun of a dog is wickedness unutterable.

To expect a cat to close the door after him or to be in by nine is hardly less so.

Malleable dog, quick cat! All the sense and knowledge and usefulness are on one side; all the calm abandon of instinct and beauty on the other. How can we possibly hope to domesticate ourselves without both? I have my cat: my dog I must go out and choose.

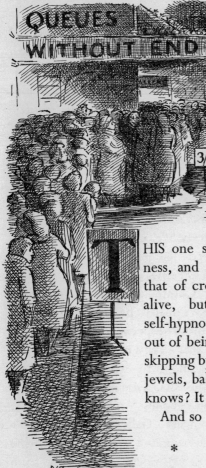

THIS one stretches away into darkness, and has an eternal look, like that of crocodiles at the zoo. It is alive, but conglomerate; awake, self-hypnotized. It gets satisfaction out of being stared at by individuals skipping by. What is it after? Crown jewels, ballet, mink, football? Who knows? It is being itself.

And so I wish it good-night.

*   *   *   *

Time was—ah youth, youth!— when I might have tagged on.

I have waited in such places as Wigmore Street on a

61

Sunday evening, with a little old woman crying 'Psychic News or Spirit World?' in the dusk.

Usually one can gauge the queue from its attendance. Thus acrobats, tearers of newspaper, barrel organs, and a voice at one's elbow quavering 'The Man who Broke the Bank at Monte Carlo' denote the precincts of cinema or theatre; coloured postcards and concertina views of London suggest Royalty, and agile haunted men with attaché cases a black market of some kind.

*   *   *   *

Not every queue, however, gets the entertainment it deserves. The House of Commons seems to me, in this respect, very badly served. Should one decide, on the spur of the moment, to drop in, one must start in Parliament Square, somewhere abreast of Cromwell, with nothing but the view to distract. What a chance, what an audience, for gasbags! Surely we owe it to Democracy that up and down that particular gutter, shaking fists or hats, should dance the I.L.P.-ite, the Inland Revenue victim, the Eaton Square Communist, the anti-vaccinationist and the pro-Proportional-Representationist, and the anarch denouncing all order, especially queues.

What happens in fact is that after a couple of hours one is beckoned up the steps and into St. Stephen's Hall. Before one stood, now one sits. One has to make the whole circuit of the hall on benches. An Iranian, perhaps, far distant, quits the Strangers' Gallery, and we all— two hundred or so—slide round a place. The marble statues of statesmen, mosaics, operatic tableaux from British history hardly come under entertainment. A secretary may scuttle, an M.P. pass: so one interprets that worn look hopeful of recognition. And this will go on indefinitely so long as there's a flicker of interest upstairs. If there's none, the Strangers' Gallery will empty a little, offering places to be filled. Either way tedium is assured.

*   *   *   *

Not that I'm against queueing: I will shuffle up to margarine counters with the next man, start outcast beyond bus shelters, glimpse over other's shoulders the last vanishing packet of —— cigarettes. This, without question, is the civilized way.

Once there were dog-fights. Now a dog can walk anywhere without fear of being pounced on; and I've no doubt the average dog is better off than he ever was.

I don't have to battle my way on buses with an umbrella or defer to fat women in post offices; and for this I am thankful.

But have I ever sung glees at night round the Oval, been the first—or even the last—to hail Murder at the Old Bailey?

*   *   *   *

One occasion sticks in my memory. It was the spring of '43. Queueing was in the air, and I found myself—over some question of priorities—in a ruly mob extending to and fro as far as the eye could see. There was a raid of sorts going on: little did we care.

'What are you here for?' I asked the old woman at my side.

'I lost me identity,' said she.

'Oh dear,' I said.

Only yesterday she'd had it.

She looked rather scared, but proud. Then a bomb went off, and we all made for shelter. Ten minutes later we had re-formed, as before.

But it wasn't many days before I had lost *mine*, and there I was back at the queue, and whom should I see but the same poor old skrimshanker.

'Good morning,' I said, stepping up beside her, 'what's the trouble this time?'

'Still me identity,' she said, 'there's complications.'

She smiled. A couple of bombs went off, and then a gas-inspector shoved his nose in, to ask what queues were for, and if I knew, why didn't I keep to them, and so on.

Then they all began shoving and elbowing, till I found my-self fifty yards further down than I'd started. Great days.

*   *   *   *

It takes six (as the old proverb says) to make a queue, and one to break it.

Beware of the threat from within: the person who worms his way up.

From the outside all queues, even little ones, are disheartening. Encourage ghost queues. Let stools do the waiting. Or why not dogs?

Avoid outpatients, those who queue all they can, queues that aren't sure which way they're going, wrong queues.

Hints to queue-breakers: come running round a corner, shouting Sinatra; scatter bribes; sing; failing everything, begin reading in loud snuffling tones the novel you have been writing about Life as it flows in and out of and round a street-corner Proust.

When you're fed up with queues, start your own. Stand by a shut door, whisper the magic word, get the thing well going, and then beetle off. In the morning, with any luck, your queue will encircle the block, without end or beginning.

*   *   *   *

I do like a wind!

At night I sleep—or wake—the better for it, for the boughs that creak, the dustbins that rattle, the moans in chimneys and charges round corners.

When I get up I may be rather disappointed that there's so little to show: not a chimney down! The houses look just as they did. But then in a window-box I notice the plant convulsively twitching; along the street comes a man—not walking but trudging air. And all through the day I'll be haunted by signs jogging, papers cavorting, the female form beautifully or comically divined, the bowler hat at last bowling away, birds hurling themselves into the current under low tear-away skies.

Then the fun will die down mysteriously as it came. Once more a terrible patience will possess people and things.

I might as well go and 'lose me identity' in a queue.

Punch Over Hampstead

SUNDAY, and the little green and red buses snail up the hill; suburban rows fall away, walls grow older and higher, trees overhang, and there we are. Where? At the seaside, it would seem, as along a promenade, in deck-chairs, holiday-makers affront the weather. Children clutch a hand and a toy or a choc-ice. Sorrowfully, round a bend, walk four donkeys. There are Punch and Judy, the sparkle of water. Not the sea, as it happens, but the Whitestone Pond;

about this headland, in a glittering haze, laps London; we are at the high point of Hampstead Heath.

While the intent small boy, our excuse for being here, watches Punch and Judy, we keep his place in the queue for a donkey. The sun plays peep-bo. A red jet-plane snarls circling on the hillside below. Where, I wonder, is that old mariner whose telescope, at tuppence a time, would envisage the tip of Southend Pier? Do carts still drive into the pond through the gangway at the end? The donkeys return and go away loaded, the queue moves up, and at last comes the donkey that's ours. I happen to know her name, Carol; she once looked in, on the way to some R.S.P.C.A. outing, to crop my lawn. We had some difficulty, I remember, in getting her out. Carol moves away, with our young friend up, and now it's *my* turn for Punch and Judy.

What a squawk! What trouncings and fellings! For a moment I wonder whether it isn't Sir Oswald Mosley (whose favourite corner this was) returned to bash us. But the melodrama is more heartfelt, and violence confined to the stage. An audience of children, squatting in front, on tiptoe, astride shoulders or goggling under elbows, follow every squeak, caper, and rap with delight. This is the life! Punch wields a frying-pan, Toby bites Punch, Punch retaliates, Punch hops and sings, Punch dies. What's this, exclaims the Doctor, how long have you been dead? Quarter of an hour, squeaks Punch. Bad, says the Doctor, I must listen to your heart; and soon he and Punch are having a fine set-to. Punch knocks the consultant dead. The Beadle (I think it must be he) appears: him also Punch kills. Then comes the Policeman, with an air of astonishment, looking everywhere for Punch except where Punch is, and demanding of the audience whether he,

67

and no one else, isn't the murderer? Yes, yells one-half—mostly girls; No, the other, mostly boys. The same fate strikes down the Policeman as the others. Now there are three corpses, slumped over the narrow frame of that stage which is all trap-door, and our old bludgeoner is in his heyday, dancing and carolling, when a very white, elusive Clown wafts in. But at this moment—the donkeys having accomplished their round—I have to break off.

All I have missed—the Baby thrown out of the window and Judy slain and Jack Ketch hanged in his own noose and the death of the Devil—I hope and don't doubt still obtains. Some of the actions and properties may have grown vestigial—a frying-pan, though where the landlord's sausages?—but the old Wickedness is at the heart of things, as once in Eden (imagine that!) and dancing aboard the Ark with a 'Hazy weather, Mr. Noah!' Nelson has tried to enlist him; he has whispered with Guy Fawkes, floored Springheel Jack. What new encounters and triumphs? Hitler, certainly, seems due, with paint to splash and a carpet to bite, and why not the Abominable Snowman? If, that's to say, today's Punch and Judy exists as more than a survival. He has roots denied to our mushroom legends of Tarzan and Mickey Mouse; but that may not be enough. From my tantalizing glimpse, I cannot be sure.

Pan pipes have gone, Scaramouch and Nobody have gone, the Crocodile and even (I believe) the Coffin have gone; can Punch remain? Curiously enough he still reveals a pristine energy on the cover of *Punch*; that magazine which till lately bore his name but so little of himself. There—for every archdeacon and schoolgirl and mothers' meeting to gaze upon—astride an ass, with a damsel in tow, he splendidly holds (you might say) his own. This great

68

indelicacy, which we owe to Dicky Doyle, so startled
the editors of the *New Yorker* that when they brought off
their famous parody of *Punch*, the cover incident quite
flummoxed them: putting him in, they left *it* out. A few
more such thwacking blows as Doyle's in the Saturnalian
cause, and we might still prevent Punch's becoming a
dummy in a museum of Great Legends.

My serious little friend, aged three, from his father's
shoulder had apparently followed the antics of Punch very
seriously indeed. He hadn't once laughed, hadn't shouted,
hadn't sung, hadn't in any way joined in, though with eyes
for everything; so that it was feared he might be too
young, as we were (outwardly at least) too old for Punch.
A second visit, then, being ruled out, we leave the puppets
for the pond, criss-crossed by yachts, speedboats, battle
cruisers, a stately two-master and a no less picturesque, if
more hardgoing, tanker. He is allowed to paddle. He
rushes in, he tries to catch a boat; and it's all his mother
can do, without falling in herself, to catch him. Whether
this is the influence of Punch, I don't know. As his socks
are being put on he cries for a moment, but already the
memory is fading, and downhill we wend along a walk
lined with a display of paintings and—sometimes preferably—the painters themselves.

At home I turn up a passage in Mayhew. Here he is, the
Punch-man of that date (about 1860) in person:

> Punch, you know, sir, is a dramatic performance
> in two hacts. It's a play, you may say. I don't think
> it can be called a tragedy hexactly; a drama is what
> we names it. There is tragic parts, and comic and
> sentimental parts, too. Some families where I
> performs will have it most sentimental—in the

original style; them families is generally sentimental theirselves. Others is all for the comic, and then I has to kick up all the games I can. To the sentimental folk I am obliged to perfirm werry steady and werry slow, and leave out all comic words and business. They won't have no ghost, no coffin, and no devil and that's what I call spilin the performance hentirely. It's the march of hintellect what's a doing all this—it is, sir.'

And looking round a world in which we over-refine with one hand and stab to the heart with the other, may we not dread lest, not only Punch, but everything else too, should go down before our 'march of hintellect'?

British Food

DREAD syllables: *food*, our bluntest four-letter word, with such associations as 'Where do we eat?', 'Think I'll go and have a bite,' and 'She's off her food (feed or grub).' What need, what possibility even, of qualifying it? Yet see how grimly and unassailably the adjective will shove in, till the whole phrase rises in all its eerie magnificence of wet lettuce, fish and bone and chips, buckskin omelette, paste sausage, blancmange, water-gravy, pea bullets, pink sponge and green stickfast, paper-thin slices of mutton, and rice mush—British Food! It was under a strange compulsion, therefore, that seeing the poster 'British Food Fair: See—Sample—Taste—Try' I made my way to Olympia.

Civilization was soon left behind. At Earl's Court a specially old and empty train crept in to take us privily to the doors. Others besides myself, a few—men with strong teeth and women with shopping bags—were entering the hall, which surprised by a nautical brightness,

like Cowes on a fine day. The commissionaire sniffed. I
sniffed. Steak and onions? No, wax, paint, and metal.

Food, however, was packed high and spread prettily in a
luxuriance of tins, jars, bottles, cartons, cellophanes,
boxes with windows, and boxes without. Many a bright
picture on a tin could we feast upon. Here were deep-
crimsoning, bulging tomatoes, here an old Highlander
picked fish with his sword, here a pig's head smiled, here
in Alpine meadows a dairymaid cradled an armful of
produce. Windmills took the skyline, and puppets danced.
And sometimes the eatables themselves, ingeniously
dovetailed, were seen. This shining pyramid, lit from
within, and displaying a few fairy-like threads in amber,
is of marmalade jars. There are jigsaws of fruit salad,
half-lobsters swathed in a lettuce leaf, biscuits and chocolates, yellow pickles, black relishes, pale shrimps. I
should like, said I, to sample a half-lobster. But lobsters
weren't forthcoming. A sausagette on a stick? My turn to
frown. 'Try,' suggested a clear housewifely voice, 'a nice
cup of coffee!' Something was poured out of a bottle;
hot water was added; milk topped it; and all I could
taste was milk. 'Quite so,' I said. But the woman next
to me, having exclaimed 'Delicious!' was already buying
the medium-sized bottle. She went on to a neighbouring
stall where Welsh Rarebits in tiny 1s. 6d. cartons were
selling briskly.

I looked at the customers—all women—and wondered.
Were they managing at home on 'one ring,' and if so how
could they afford the labour-saving price? Did they lack
time, touch, taste, a husband, or what? An energy far
greater than mine for prising open lids and screw tops
they certainly possessed.

Elsewhere the curious were discovering Pepsicola at the

correct temperature, examining the pastry concocted from bread and marge, and (I don't quite know what it was doing here) touring a gallery of the Queen's childhood in photographs. Real turtles, in a large hexagonal tank, flapped ceremoniously like the aldermen to whom they are devoted. A placard caught at me: 'Ham and Tongue Together for the First Time!' For the first time? How many years had I gone on playing cricket for their sake? But a closer inspection revealed one of those cylindrical moulds whose only demerit is that every mouthful must taste exactly like the next; whereas, with tongue—ox-tongue—the delight is to stray from creamy bit to streaky, to vary the melting granularity of fat with firm toothable rind . . . but why labour it? Such sensualities are not of our time and place; in our meals, like the old *Criterion* writers, we strive always towards a synthesis. Spong or toham strikes the authentic note. A new T. L. Peacock should be busy inscribing the prandiologues that arise out of cocktail, tinned viand and frozen veg.

What philosophical diatribe, for example, or convivial song would greet the arrival of the

'Baked Coconut Flavoured Semolina Pudding: 1 pint of milk, 1½ ozs. Three Graces Coconut Flavoured Semolina, 2-3 tablespoonfuls of sugar, ½ oz. margarine. Place the Three Graces Semolina . . . '?

I needn't go on. This recipe comes from the catalogue which describes itself as being also a cookery book. Lyrics such as the above will fascinate the food-ridden. I shouldn't choose, myself, except on a desert island, to live long by Olympia standards; in fact one of the rare dishes here that makes me look impatiently at the clock is Paella Valenciana offered by Stand 144, 'Products of Spain.' It and the Dutch exhibit, relegated very properly to a gallery among hardware, jewellery, disinfectants, and patent mincers, gives us our only, as it were, naked contact with Food. What! Real cheeses, real eggs, real butter! Perhaps they aren't real, but they look it, and not frosty brightness but a warm smile stays the passer-by.

Desert island: of course, if we were Swiss Family Robinson, all the Olympia products could be washed ashore after us by the genius of shipwreck. And perhaps that's just what we are, desert-islanders with a patent can-opener, and our only alternative raw or British cookery.

Homeward bound, I missed my way and fell in with a tea-shop or café. It had been open, I suppose, since 8 a.m. serving the uninterrupted meal in which breakfast, dinner, tea, and supper were rolled into one. Now late lunchers were merging with early tea-timers, rock-salmon with crumble cake; urn-coffee, tea from the bag quelled any stomach that might take a wrong turn, and over all a calm indigestion reigned. Many, sitting in caps and hats and coats, seemed desperately ready—but for what? The look in their eyes—unless I'm much mistaken—said: *British food for the British; we can take it.*

Beautiful Odd Fish

HEY inhabit a world of their own. You notice them in a recess by the window, where a shaft of sunlight penetrates: Zebras, Swordtails, Rosy Barbs, and a rarer specimen of Black Molly or Platy. There are fifty of them, more or less, the tiniest (born yesterday) a semolina grain with eyes and a tail, the largest a roving three-inch giant. These glinty strangers reveal an astonishing variety of colours as they approach, and the colour is volatile. For a passing moment the sun patch will rob them of vividness. They're no longer jewels; silver armour is pierced, electric-blue sheen shows its blood lining. A greenish semi-transparence has brought back homelier waters. 'So you keep fish,' remarks the visitor, moving in the direction of the tank. Then the light-switch is pressed. Delicately, extravagantly, the whole picture floods up or rather down, from its top lighting—yellow gravel, emerald foliage, white or pink rocks, and the fish yet again tinted with a pale golden translucency—a Douanier Rousseau in movement and depth.

That picture, while never changing its nature, rearranges itself from instant to instant. Within the confines—twenty-four inches, say, by twelve by fifteen—the exquisitely painted figures are always coming and going, joining in schools, whisking off, chasing one another, looking out sideways, nosing, gliding, hovering, wriggling. The impression is one of idyllic employment. Many movements suggest a skating scene, with such a mingling of lacka-daisical precision and smooth idleness, such figurings, but that here the evolutions are three-dimensional. A figure of eight stands on its head; the winning approach is down a moon-beam; speed merchants, having dazzled with their exploits, poise themselves negligently in space. The gracefulness which a pair of skates will bestow upon you or me (supposing we can employ them) comes to the fish from his element. Water resists, water buoys up; he lazes by right, and a spine quiver ending in the tail will twang him arrow-like wherever he may wish. Zebras, for example, those jersey-striped racers of the fish-tank, can dash round and round and in and out like mad greyhounds. They exchange ellipses for straight lines, and pull up dead: even their angularities please. It is not till sickness inter-feres with a most delicate sense of balance, consisting of ear-stones in sacs, that we realize how controlled and fine are the actions we take for granted. A mad Nijinsky is hardly a more lamentable sight than the fish gone groggy.

There are lulls but no pauses in the life of this warm, watery cubicle. Its behaviour is determined largely by the search for oxygen and food and by the sex-cycle of attraction, union, and birth. Plants supply oxygen, and are themselves sustained by the carbon-dioxide liberated by the fish; feeding includes small water fleas (the *daphnia* of our ponds), smaller brine-shrimps, worms white and red, and various commercial meals. The sex habits of tropical fish are both more urgent and more fanciful than one might expect. Millions of Rainbow fish (now known as Guppies, after their popularizer, Dr. Plantaganet Lechmere Guppy) present an almost uninterrupted spectacle of the love chase, with the little rainbow-coloured male in pursuit, tail-waggling for the position from which he can dart in: a satisfaction, it would seem, always denied, yet in the year a pair of Guppies will proliferate some 800 young. By contrast the courtship of Swordtails is a duel, a flash of knitting needles. With Gouramis the male wraps himself round the female in a close embrace. Catfish tickle each other's necks. Rasboras mate in groups. Angel fish are faithful unto death.

Even more remarkable are the circumstances attending birth. Eggs may be glued in clusters on leaves, embedded in bubbles, carried in the mouth of the male, dropped between pebbles or into sediment on the tank floor, or placed above water and carefully splashed. Live-bearers hatch their young internally. The living fish, one of a hundred or two, will perhaps be born folded double, to straighten itself and seek an air bubble from the surface, if not eaten by parents or others on the way; for cannibalism presents no problem to creatures so multitudinous, though in many species the male will defend eggs from a fruitful and hungry spouse.

But not all the goings-on of the tropical aquarium are dictated by hunger and sex. Fish play. When they are well, they enjoy the free movement most natural to them, and there are antics that can come only from exuberance. One such antic is a dance in which the fish makes a series of lightning rolls or frisks along the gravel bed, rubbing first one flank and then the other, and giving the general effect of a stone at ducks-and-drakes that has suddenly become aware of its performance. Sensuousness is by no means absent from the fish world. To judge from their dances and courtships—movements quite as expressive as bird-song—they enjoy more contacts than we suppose. Their most acute sense is that of touch, and they feel distant objects by changes of pressure along a sensitive line running from nose to tail. I should say, from a brief idle observation, that the happy fish exults at least as much as the cat on the tiles, the sky-plumbing lark, the bat at twilight, or the seal juggling with a beach-ball.

Though captive, these delicate pigmies (few of whom can have known their native waters) introduce none of the pathos that usually haunts captivity. Their glass walls, against which they nose thoughtfully, and at times even in ecstasy, seem to belong less to a prison than to some airily designed play-room. They look out, as into a foggy day. They don't know us. Boredom hasn't touched them, and danger hardly exists. They may have been bred in Stockwell and nourished in North Finchley—neither redolent of the Yangtse Kiang or the Amazon—and their bright water-world may be fantastically unlike nature, but given warmth, food, light, and air, they will thrive.

My own favourite of the moment is the Catfish (*Corydorus paleatus*). His spreckly green-brown with mother-of-pearl lights obviously corresponds closely with some

South American pebble ground, for it's his habit when surprised to lie quite still. Instinct persuades him that he is invisible. I look at him; he looks at me. But I can play at this waiting game too; and after a while, seeing no movement, he will resume his activity. All glitter and accoutrement, jangling (as it were) scales, barbels, and fins, he comes hurrying along the sands like some whiskered Chinese knight late for battle. He is plump. He stands on his head. He wriggles. What can he be up to? Digging for titbits, it seems. A bubble or two may escape him during these exertions, and suddenly he will fly to the surface himself, first making sure there's nobody looking, and *stealing* his mouthful of air, as though it were a cream bun at a window. To the other inhabitants of the aquarium he pays scant attention; they find him, though not disagreeable, too burly for playing tricks on. He can also —rare aptitude!—close his eye, and since his usual outlook is one of serious fuss varied by watchful immobility, the wink comes as a surprise.

Fish character goes largely by kind; and in the books on the subject—Innes's *Exotic Aquarium Fishes*, for example— will be found hundreds of kinds almost as diverting to read about as to encounter. There is *Copeina*, already referred to, whose eggs are laid out of water, so that several days have to be spent in splashing them; *Anableps* has double eyes for seeing above and below the surface while swimming; *Pterois volitans*, waving tentacle fins, hypnotizes its victims; the savage *Piranha* will bite lumps out of the hand that feeds; while many others, such as *Rivulus strigatus* and *Sheepshead Lebia*, attract by rumours of beauty. Fork-tailed Paradise Fish, Climbing Perch, Mud Springer, Fighting Fish and Croaking Fish seem no less fascinating than their names. But of course, one's own fish are best.

79

What is their appeal? The dreamy, intent preoccupation of a universe in miniature, of live butterflies in a case, of a real ship in a bottle pitching through stormy seas. Where the Victorian glass paper-weight could feign a snowstorm, this prism perpetuates its make-believe. Its outdoors is our indoors: we can approach, we can hardly imagine such a bright, womb-like existence as this contained by water. It communicates its own lucidity of beauty and silence.

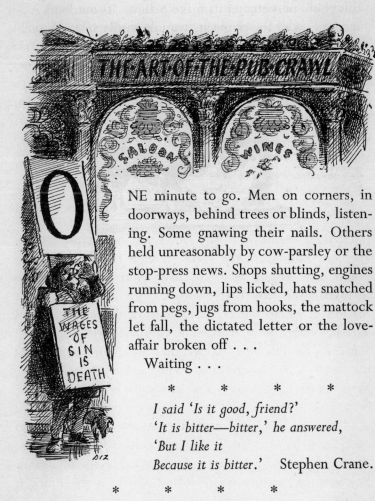

THE ART OF THE PUB-CRAWL

SALOON

WINES &

THE WAGES OF SIN IS DEATH

ONE minute to go. Men on corners, in doorways, behind trees or blinds, listening. Some gnawing their nails. Others held unreasonably by cow-parsley or the stop-press news. Shops shutting, engines running down, lips licked, hats snatched from pegs, jugs from hooks, the mattock let fall, the dictated letter or the love-affair broken off . . .

Waiting . . .

*   *   *   *

I said 'Is it good, friend?'
'It is bitter—bitter,' he answered,
'But I like it
Because it is bitter.'   Stephen Crane.

*   *   *   *

The year has brought reports from conquerors of earth sea, and sky. With Everest climbed, the Amazon's source cannot remain much longer hidden. Here's Mr. Haroun Tazieff, who last year delicately hung on the lips of volcanoes (*Craters of Fire*), now plumbing cold rock in the Pyrenees (*Caves of Adventure*). Mr. Philip Wills, gliding champion and author of *On Being a Bird*, roams with vultures and scales the heights of cumulo-nimbus. Bubble-men who have chased sharks and danced with octopuses outvie one another like acrobats; others wriggle their way barking into seals' breeding-grounds, or boldly introduce ants to the drawing-room.* To say nothing of the steeplejacks, sewer-hunters, parliamentary committee men, nudists, ostrich riders, and Egyptian Channel swimmers, all agog with a new consciousness.

—What's yours? A dog's nose, cold.

*   *   *   *

Of their company is Mr. Athelstan Shad, pub-crawler. He does not reject the term, though tabernologist—he points out—would seem to cover more of the interests involved. We may have jaunted, without insisting; not Mr. Shad. He trumpets the passions of the spree. He has dared greatly. In a succession of adventures, of which *Whose Round*, *Pints of Difference*, and *More Inns and Outs* are the chief, he has assorted a taste and experience all his own. What he doesn't know about drinking ways, old and new, isn't worth knowing. Our understanding of *'onkh*, the elaborate sconcing system of the middle Pharaohs, owes everything to Mr. Shad; and it was he who discovered, under a tree-stump in Barra, the original recipe for mead. Yet another mystery was resolved when, at the Linnean

---

* There are—we learn from Mr. Morley Wragge's *Ants* (1953)—houses in Eastbourne where the dreaded Argentine ant is, welcome or not, a guest.

Society in 1939, he demonstrated the making of bees' wine from bees.

His new book *Publand* (Red Lion Press, 42s.) is generous as its theme. It is, in fact, the guide-book and testament we have been looking for, indispensable to pub-crawlers of whatever shade. A glance at the index will reveal its encyclopædic nature:

> 'Mechanical pianos, extant—still in use; Alcoholism among Commissioners of Oaths (figures since 1817); Zymurgy, whither now; Tankard, collapsible, for hat; Camels, extraordinary effect of cider on; Libation rites in Rotherhithe; Pubs, aerial—*v*. Sky Platform; Sipping, disastrous consequences of; and Fields, W.C., a revaluation, with some unpublished bouts.'

—Thick again, look at it!—End of the barrel.—Yesterday, it was the new barrel: who gets the middle?

* * * *

It is some years since Mr. Shad let his cat out of the bag. This was, of course, the bicycle. To many, for whom the Pub Crawl always had been and always would be a Crawl, to be undertaken ceremoniously on foot, it seemed outlandish, an anomaly, a deliberate flouting of tradition.

Why a bicycle? Siphons squirted, mugs were topped up. The war came. 'This will put an end to his tricks,' they said. But did it? His runs between Greenwich and Harlesden brought him fame. 'Will Shad come through?' it was asked, with the bombs dropping round; and always he did.

Of course, pubs weren't pleasant places in those days, especially corner ones.

* * * *

Why a bicycle? Because, explained Mr. Shad, you can fall off.

His case against the old style of Crawl—set out here at length—is that it is a contradiction in terms. Alcohol transports and should give sinew to imagination and action. The pedestrian, notoriously unable to pass a lighted doorway, goes far too slow, gets nowhere, and ends, hopelessly fuddled, in the street where he started. A horse might help, but will certainly fall into bad habits, such as taking his master home, insensible. The horse—according to Mr. Shad—leads directly to excess. And not much better is the tricycle, neither satisfying with its speed nor unmistakably rejecting an unworthy rider.

Only the bicycle goes fast, flatters no one, is mobile and sensitive, and—an important stage in Mr. Shad's argument—exacts just the right degree of effort to counteract drift.

The secret, he reveals, is not to tarry long, thus imbibing the insidious poison of others' drinks,* and to match intake with exercise. With care† the required balance may be preserved over considerable periods of time.

*   *   *   *

He has been everywhere and seen everything—including a mirage of the Eiffel Tower on the Brighton Road—but to London he returns again and again. The twinkle of lights in the fog, the saloon bar empty except

* Is it generally known that cirrhosis of the liver is an occupational disease of waiters, who acquire it not by drinking but from fumes inhaled in the course of their duties? (For a discussion of this, see the *New Survey of London Life and Labour*, 1939.)

† Intake and exercise. Two miles per pint, or sixteen miles to the gallon, will offer a fair working average, though the figures are only approximate, depending on the individual and on circumstances; a heat-wave may reduce the m.p.g. to ten, and cool wet weather extend it to forty or fifty.

for two borough councillors under a palm tree, draw him irresistibly. Dawn in a beer-house at Covent Garden; unruffled summer in the Tavern at Lord's, with only the faint chink of ice on glass to disturb the afternoon; the sad singers at Collins's or the Metropolitan seen, but not heard, from a side-long bar; Christmas with its fairylights and merry little attaché-cases and paper-chains; sherry and *The Times* in Holborn, frescoes and alfrescoes at Islington; the first day of Burton; shag smoke at Dirty Dick's rising under the crocodile; that landlord in Hampstead who, after the doors had closed, would fling all dirty glasses down the cellar steps, whence they would be collected at the end of the week; nights under the stars, in a wheelbarrow: such memories cannot but moisten the eye, and bring a quick swallow.

*   *   *   *

The second-hand comes full circle. Across streets, over greens and valleys, can be heard the shuffle, the shooting of bolts.

A million men wait, take a step forward.

They're open! Half-past five! We're off!

The adventure—the quest of a new consciousness—starts.

Hound Trail

RARELY going to the Dogs, which quite take the sting out of it, I found myself recently at the Hounds.

Do you know them? They are of that ilk which, with us, mobs foxes, but up there—up in Cumberland—they race the fells. Almost the first thing that met us meandering in third through Matterdale was this thoroughbred; tall and thin, mild, pale in coffee-and-cream. He was introduced as Wyndham Lad, puppy, and more than a fair chance. One melting look, and the back of the car was his for the afternoon.

The morning—one of those pin-bright mornings, with snail-trails of water on the hills—we had spent castling. Square and strong stood Dacre, but with a farmer tenant. We rang: no answer from those halls where once met the three kings, Athelstan, Constantine, and Owain. Away, we were told, at Butlin's; not for several nights or days would the wireless roar to the rafters.

86

So off we bounced, forgetting the wild Dacres and a churchyard mystery of four bears, to talk puppies and maidens, hounds, past, present, and to come.

We passed a charabanc, and there they were, crowding into a high field—men, women, and children, in cars or vans, on motor-bikes and on foot, bookies with blackboards, a policeman, a canteen or two, five hundred people in all, with some seventy hounds. These were being walked to and fro, or sheltered under a wall, the afternoon having turned cold. Our own hound was quickly lost in the throng. He might win—this seemed common opinion—but only if he could get over his habit of looking round at the finish. We backed him, not heavily, at 8 to 1.

Then there was a stir, a drift downfield; wild music starting; the runners lined up, each with his owner behind; all eyes on the gate through which after a while would appear the trailer with his aniseed-and-paraffin rag which he has dragged five miles. This course, up hill and down dale, will be covered in under twenty minutes. The trailer slouches up through the grass, and the handkerchief jerks down; they're off, round and past the trailer, over the wall, through the trees, gone. Now's the time to watch odds, crunch pies, swallow scalding tea, and attend the prognostications and sightings of those who know every grass-blade and hound-hair.

We pick up a few things. Most owners are labourers, navvies from the coast. Rules are rigid, each man keeping an eye on the next, but even so there are tricks; witness this small green van dashing off down the road, followed. Hound trails have so gripped the Lakelander that at the height of the season there may be twenty or thirty a week —or none at all, following a bad case of sheep-worrying.

All field-glasses, now, and a telescope are trained on

some altitude of the fell behind. Such asides as 'The beck'll sort them out' or 'Black Diamond's fifth' make us stare, but in vain. We stamp our feet, lean backs to the wind that is pulling mist over a crag and whisking off the last rents of sunlight. Mayberries in the hedges, and the heather merging with the cut bracken . . . season nearly over . . .

Suddenly, incredibly along the high sky-line are seen specks moving; they descend, silhouettes become dots on the green, flick over a wall, slant down a field with a rock; the rock explodes—sheep, sheep scattering; but the long irregular string of hounds (as one can now just envisage them) trails on, till a near hill intervenes. I swear the leader is light-coloured. Everybody strolls towards that starting-point which is also the finish.

Owners are lined up. Judges clump. The crowd pushes and exclaims. Someone's pointing. 'Catchers, on your marks!' and from the waiting rank comes such a cater-wauling of yells, whistles, screams, oaths and endearments, with much dancing and fluttering of handkerchiefs, as must surely signal the advent of Mr. Bevan himself.

When the leader is almost up to us he wavers, caught between the hullabaloo ahead and the press behind, seeming quite nonplussed.

'Come on!' I yell, 'it's *him!*'

And more wafted than winning he's over. Ten minutes later he sits, cloaked like a granny, in the car.

We are proud, even a little richer, as we drive off with next season's hope—if only he won't *look back*.

I shall return to the Lakes: their wild splendours and veilings, and the obstinate humours of the inhabitants, whose green speech matches their bacon, are not to be resisted. Anyone wishing to substantiate himself with them

88

seems to have a choice of ways. He may grow lean with the hounds, or fat with sheep.

Curiously, what haunts me most is the fell sheep, a very different fellow from your southdown cosies, tough, alien, dark, Celtic perhaps; though, as he squats under a rock watching cars pass, the face is Disraeli's. With him—and, say, four thousand nine hundred and ninety-nine others— would go a nice subsidy of £1,500 a year.

London Backs

E were dawdling along that stretch of canal which runs a mysterious vein through Regent's Park; ripe blackberries overhung the water, a weeping willow hinted at Renoir, chestnuts and planes with their top branches alight found deep down another, negative sky: all ahead of us was sunlight and shadow, unbroken liquidity, into which we lazily thrust, nibbling at an inverted landscape, corkscrewing trees and concertinaing bridges . . . .

The thrill—the unmitigated thrill—may need a little explaining. Everywhere on summer evenings it is delightful to idle under trees on water: here it was a delight for so long unattainable as to have given rise to a different kind of pleasure. How often, from a park walk or one of the foot-bridges, have not Londoners stared down into the seclusion of this waterway? Its half-wildness, its secrecy startle. We would halt, smoke a cigarette or drop stones. Time yawned. Once in a while we might hear the chug-chug of a barge round the corner or (along that path to which there's no entrance) watch a horse shouldering, a gang of urchins who, having breached the wire, were after adventure; soon their cries and sallies were swallowed up.

Privacy had come to us in a public park; we were in London, and worlds away from it; we had escaped the geometry of streets to retain—with a strange fascination, if we didn't dwell on it—the faint traffic mumble. And winter would bring an even lovelier isolation of black trees, snow patches, curling mists. At the moment that's hardly thinkable, except that this scene always wears a half-legendary look, less of nature than of art, as though some landscapist, tired of conventional follies and back window avenues, had created here the *trompe l'œuil* of a lifetime. The barge that had taken ten minutes to dwindle out of sight would itself seem slightly unreal.

Thus the spell-bending: which I had known since first, as a child, I gazed down through the bridge railings. Actually to descend, to participate or guiltily explore, no more occurred to me than to join the huntsmen of Breughel's 'Winter' or take a bite at one of Van Gogh's apples. There followed, it is true, years in which I thought of hiring a canoe to make the journey across London from some point near Twyford Abbey to Limehouse reach. But my plan, or fantasy, never materialized. 'Canal, Regent's Park' remained for me a picture by an unknown master; until, a few weeks ago, I discovered, with something of a shock, that passenger trips along this very stretch were a regular thing, having started in the Festival year. As soon as I could I hurried to Blomfield Road (Ruskin's 'Little Venice,' within the arms of Edgware and Harrow Roads), where at ninety-minute intervals the narrow boat *Jason* leaves on its eastward journey.

I have taken my seat, I look round at the passengers (a good sprinkling), at the painted cabin, the dark water, the buildings luckier just here in their view than in themselves. Others are doing the same: the spectacled, chubby,

middle-aged lady in a print dress, who invariably graces
such outings, has her sketch-book ready; Bognor seems
to have been her last visit. We smile, devotees of the
picturesque, if not yet at one another. Soon, with a final
attendance on latecomers and a rope hauled in, we are off,
imperceptibly off, for the long tunnel, through which a
few old horse-barges have still to be poled from the ceiling
while the horse is led overland: half an hour's toil to them,
three minutes' thrill to us. The small end with its bright
green vision lets us out past weeds and sparse banks, power
station coolers, goods yards, iron foundries; we slide
under roads and railways; a train rushes across, but we go
on neither pausing nor hurrying, negotiating bends, taking
the middle, meeting nobody; and then all at once, with
the banks growing steep and green, Regent's Park is above
us.

Enchantment—if to me eerily disenchanting—is ours.
We dawdle in eternity. The feeling that I've broken some
understanding, that I'm now part of it, gathers accom-
plices. Thin, lonely men (very different from the stalwarts
along the Seine) sit fishing behind bushes and in the nook
of walls—for roach, so they say, but it might be octopuses
or moon fish; they have been here for hours, for life; near
one is a gaunt dog curled asleep. They make way for us
with a sort of reluctant delicacy. Occasionally the water
slaps against stone steps (these are for the benefit of horses
that may have slipped in), a bough falls, a milk-bottle is
left rocking. Under the bridges we crawl forward, and
now I, who so often looked down, am looked down on. A
plum stone, or some such object, is even dropped on me.
We *are* intruders, and as such we pass through the zoo,
catching glimpses of pea-hens and ponies, jungle cock,
antelope, and the stranger people these animals are looking

at. Rather hastily we look at one another. Small boys don't hesitate to point or to yell 'You're sinking.' However, we survive to angle the dilapidation of Chalk Farm with its hollyhock rows, ruined church, distillery windows, and then, before the first lock, we turn back. I shall look forward, if ever I realize my canoe, to the stage beyond which would take in the forlorn beauties of Islington.

On the journey home our captain, a young painter energetically making ends meet, points to landmarks and oddities: Blow-up Bridge, so called from the barge of explosives that long ago burst its central arch, and now distinguished by eight iron Doric columns; Grove House gardens, so well barbered and shaved in front on its St. John's Wood corner, but showing a dirty neck to the water; a cricket-bat factory to remind us of Lord's, with New Zealand planks weathering on a roof; the house spanning the canal where lurks a Chief Inspector of Scotland Yard ('Must have read Simenon,' observes the shrewd plump lady in the print dress, whose drawings have been of the sketchiest). Here, we are told, resided G. H. Elliott; there we overtake a duck with two ducklings. We come to our tunnel again, we probe its mystery, wondering what would happen if an opposing narrow boat chose to enter, we take a turn about 'Little Venice'—that pool with an island, where the Grand Union canal strikes off—and so back to earth.

Over the Hedge

G OOD heavens—Candide! Is it really you?'

'None other.'

'And still, I see, cultivating your garden.'

'Yes, I'm afraid I've rather lived on that last line of Voltaire's. But think what a splendid opening it will make for the sequel—should that ever be written. "He was cultivating his garden when the first atom bomb fell."'

'First *and* last sentence, it seems to me.'

'Not necessarily. The second might read: "It deprived

him of both legs, one arm, and an eye; but soon, with the aid of a couple of sticks and a hook, he was going about his business among men." '

'Admirable! But what brought you to England?'

'Oh, the usual thing: like everyone else I'd fought in too many wars, on too many sides. When it was all over, and I had collected sundry decorations including an Iron Cross and the Order of the Golden Giraffe, I looked for the new world in Russia, where first I swept streets, and then was entrusted with the task of rewriting the history of Bulgaria. This led to my arrest, on the charge of infringing truth. I was transferred to the salt-mines. Every morning we would set to with smiles, work being, as it was said, the joy of life. So it went on for four years.'

'My poor Candide, how you must have suffered!'

'Then one day I pointed to one of our guards and said "This gloomy man, who has never worked in his life, is paid fifty times more than we." In the general confusion I slipped off, and after many adventures made my way to America. We steamed into New York harbour in the dawn. With what delight did I watch the sun rise on the Statue of Liberty! All day I walked about the streets, the tall streets, head in the air, and at evening came on a patriot addressing a crowd. Everyone, he was insisting, should be examined for his opinions, free of charge, as he would be for tuberculosis or cancer, and so the State would enjoy permanent good health. "Wonderful," I exclaimed to the man standing beside me, "are the ways of God's own country!" He put me under arrest—to save me, as he said, from the attentions of the crowd—and I was carried off to Ellis Island, where through the bars I enjoyed an excellent view of that same Lady of Liberty, with her back to me.

95

'I made friends with a Chinaman, who had raised an enormous family in Minneapolis but could not disguise the fact that he was Chinese, and when our deportation orders came through we struck out for Plymouth in a rowing-boat with which an Englishman had set his mind on crossing the Atlantic. During that voyage, which was not without adventure, we enjoyed such freedom of conscience as I have never known before or since; and in fact as soon as we sighted land the Englishman wished to go on and encircle the globe. My friend and I, thanking him, swam ashore, just in time to appear as wrecked Spaniards in a pageant; Drake was finishing his game of bowls, and all the town was there, with pipers and the Mayor disporting himself among bathing girls: as jolly a reception as you could imagine. And so I settled in England; where I am known, by the way, as Mr. White. But enough of these trifles, what do you think of my magnolia?'

'Exquisite. Tell me, though——'

'It's lemon-scented. My ideal, of course, is the herbaceous border—what do we not owe to Robinson?—with bearded peonies, dog flax, giant urticaria. And roses: these are white Damask and yellow purple Tuscany. Did you go to the Chelsea Flower Show?'

'I was taken.'

'My Boguljubovs won a prize: a third, there was strong competition. But did you ever see such an efflorescence? What gorgeousness—what wealth! The streets of El Dorado were nothing to it.'

'Perhaps; but——'

'But, you would say, the simple old-fashioned blooms are best? Nothing, I agree, could be more charming than —look at them!—those two cabbage-whites executing their *pas de deux*, wavery-papery over the foxgloves. And

wallflowers! But at the ball they mustn't be all wallflowers.
. . . My roses need a little watering—ah, the roses and
raptures, as your poet says, of Noisettiana——'

'Answer me, I beg, one thing. In your unrivalled
experience of the world, of many ages and many climes,
do you find humanity today worse or better?'

'How can you ask! Why in the Westphalia of my childhood—delightful and instructive though that was—we were
heathens: no one had so much as heard of Pentstemon!'

'Possibly. But mankind itself, with its wars, its Hitlers
and Stalins, its atom bombs——'

'No shadows without light.'

'You believe that? Then I suspect you have been talking
to Pangloss. By the way, how is the old gentleman?'

'My poor master?—a mere shadow of himself: you may
see him any Sunday afternoon addressing the crowd in
Hyde Park.'

'All, however, is for the best?'

'Naturally; though of late he has been much fired by
possibilities of travel to Mars or Venus.'

'I should have thought his experience of the last, at any
rate, already sufficient.'

'It's our duty, he argues, to enjoy the best of all possible
universes.'

'His destiny was always to travel far. And how is
Cunég—er, Mrs. White?'

'Remarkably well. She keeps to her bed, thus conserving
her energies—''

'Another philosophy!'

'—and her hearing has grown very acute.'

'Then I'll whisper.'

'There's no need; so long as she can hear spade or
clippers—but let that stop for an instant——'

'I understand. How does she take to the idea of your memoirs?'

'She has yet to learn of them. When she does, she will undoubtedly—even at her age—insist on my teaching her to read.'

'*Candide*, Part II—the genuine Part II—that's a pleasure I'd not even dreamed of. I shall certainly look forward to reading you!'

'Then you'll be lucky. All my readers, now I come to think of it, will be men and women of extraordinary good fortune.'

'Of course, can one's readers be otherwise?'

'You misunderstand me. My meaning is that in the best of all possible existences, as Pangloss will not fail to point out, everybody will owe his or her survival to the special dispensation of providence. Was ever humanity so blessed before?'

'And meanwhile you will trim privet and collect cups with your roses?'

'I shall endeavour.'

'Long may you continue to do so.'

Where's Raleigh's Cloak?

A S I walked down Oxford Street in the afternoon—no, as I affronted, shoved, shouldered, eeled my way through, disrupting families, snapping window spells—I was thankful for the bill in my pocket. '*Calling all London!*' it began: I had studied it on the bus, before quitting the bus.

Cooks' Sons, Dukes' Sons, Sons of a Millionaire!
To the
EXHIBITION
From Elizabeth to Elizabeth
To be held at
Hutchinson House, Stratford Place, W.1.
Weekdays from 10 a.m.—6.p.m. Sundays from
2 p.m.—6 p.m., etc.

Stratford Place, that alcove on the north side which offers a refreshing side-glance to the herd, appeared soon between Lilley & Skinner and Dolcis; parked cars huddle its quiet, but one can't, within a barrow-boy's spit from Oxford Street, expect everything. The house at the end, under Hutchinson's adoption, retains much elegance from Adam and Flaxman.

No sign of an Exhibition. Having called us, it holds its peace. Doubtfully we mount steps, push open a door: behind it, a lady nods, smiles, tears off a ticket. No (whole-hearted smile), no catalogues till tomorrow. And now which door? I try one and am directed to another. An inner hall sends up a staircase, which loftily we ascend; and the door opposite is ours.

We are there. But then comes the question, *where*? The problem is to find a starting-point. I glance right and left: on one side there's an illuminated text of the Gospel according to St. John, on the other a case dedicated to Baden-Powell. Should I take the first, I come to photographs of the Victorian great, extending indefinitely, it would seem, in recession of time. Baden-Powell, then? But it is hard, for the non-Scout, to gauge what prospect that little wood statue, surrounded by medals and badges, could open up.

So I forge ahead into the close-packed middle of Elizabethan seals and parchments, the New World, snapshots of tricyclists well-met (to which I shall certainly return), a glowing map of enemy Scotland, musical autographs, and arrive at the doorway to Costume. Here is breathing-space, amplitude: at once the attention is frisked by a row of Edwardian stockings, embroidered, starred, flowered, fluted, and one pair yellow unashamedly —perhaps the retort to a more serious aunt's blue. Parasols, silk slippers; two gossipy blinker bonnets of about 1820 on either side of a tapering hatted beau, and a sack dress from our own twenties; some naval peacockery or other; a cake shape, but a so glistly, thistly, feathery delight of a hat when one knows who wore it—Queen Victoria; then the same monarch's 'day dress,' to bring shivers to prison matrons; a ballroom vision of 1889, all spangles, butterflies, rose-trees with the roses sewn on—no need for its wearer to seek the conservatory, she's there; knickers and corsets and gloves and pink or blue breakfast bonnets. At that moment, on the wall, almost life-size, I catch sight of a lion tearing at the back of a horse. Startled, I hurry out.

I am on a landing. Shock succeeds shock. A diminutive model of Stephenson's Rocket leads to Gleep—well named—the first Graphite Low Energy Experimental Pile; this is surmounted on the wall behind by a sort of Declaration of Atomic Rights in bold lettering; but underneath, and behind Gleep, hangs a portrait gallery (photographs of prints) of twenty-four worthies ranging from Richard Steele to Blanche Parry, Welsh Maid-of-Honour to Elizabeth I, and Wilson, the landscape painter to Richard Recorde, who introduced algebra to England. He also, we are told, invented the sign $=$. I must admit that I doubted this when the next two objects met my eye, one being a tiny De Havilland Comet and the other a giant Craigmillar, winner of the St. Leger in 1875. What were they doing there? What was anything doing there? 'Where,' I heard a voice in the distance, 'is the main part of the Exhibition?' No reply. I looked fearfully round: a cross-section of a windmill, an empty tea-room, a letter from Lewis Carroll, some cameos, a vision of pink flats in Paddington, and a dark, disappearing stairway met my inquiry. I started to descend the last, but turned back. A corridor with a predominantly Welsh flavour and a room of first editions and manuscripts—among which a page from De Quincey's *Autobiographic Sketches* was balanced by a Marie Stopes sonnet, unalterably majestic in pencil, ink and print— brought me back to Baden-Powell and the point from which I had set out. More, far more than three rooms, a landing, and a corridor had been traversed in the meanwhile. I felt for the handbill in my pocket. 'COME and SEE——'

The lights went out.

When they came back I read: 'COME and SEE a Short History of the British People in Outline . . . . ' What? Short History? British People? Outline? A cool, feminine voice in the next room was saying, 'Of course, we change the dresses,' and with the lights off again, and on again, this time for good, I expected everything to have changed. But, remarkably, nothing had. The lion tore the horse in the boudoir; four Welsh authors were encased over a marble hand-basin; Dr. Stopes still rhymed; Blanche Parry and Gleep and Craigmillar nestled ever closer together. The landing *collage*, in fact, after several revisits, I came to regard as the masterpiece here, radiating a weird significance through the rooms and out into Stratford Place, where before the front steps was an empty space marked 'Hutchinson Car.'

A last happy half-hour was spent with Victorian street life, in photographs, some well known, from the Gernsheim collection. If only John Thomson and Adolphe Smith and their camera had existed a little earlier, to be able to go the rounds with Mayhew! The Italian musicians with a harp were new to me, the club-footed doctor peddling cures, the junk-shop on a corner superbly lit; then old sepia prints of old buildings; then Great Victorian heads, and how admirably self-dramatized they were, and how many! Carlyle, side-face, anticipates a D. H. Lawrence grown grey and old; Fox Talbot looks the black-and-white wizard he was; a pellucid strangeness is Beardsley's; Hardy, with a beard, needs re-reading; and Mr. Sidney Webb shows up not merely as a Chekhov character but as Chekhov himself.

There are, I hope I have made plain, rocks of enchantment to which even the most bewildered can cling; or that Outline (which exists at least in the minds of the All Arts' Committee of the National Playing-fields Association) may be thrillingly and ineffectually hunted; or one can slide and pause, pause and slide, mingling with sense such sweets of surrealism as rarely come a Londoner's way.

So, cooks' sons, dukes' sons, sons of a millionaire, leave your Oxford Street of maundering footsteps, jammed buses, bubble trails, kerb howls, nylon twists, and roll up to quiet Stratford Place, where every day from ten to six the moon shines bright!

Lunch-Time Prophet

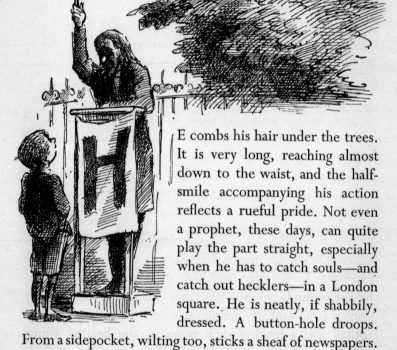

E combs his hair under the trees. It is very long, reaching almost down to the waist, and the half-smile accompanying his action reflects a rueful pride. Not even a prophet, these days, can quite play the part straight, especially when he has to catch souls—and catch out hecklers—in a London square. He is neatly, if shabbily, dressed. A button-hole droops. From a sidepocket, wilting too, sticks a sheaf of newspapers.

Lunch-time in Lincoln's Inn Fields—since 1376 a 'common walking or sporting place for the citizens of London'—offers its usual diversions: to jousting-grounds have succeeded tennis courts, and if public hangings and

104

robbery by violence no longer tickle the multitude, there are netball, open-air snacks, and prophecy.

He combs his hair. He sky-gazes. He winks (so it seems) sleepily into his beard. Pink faces pass, turn, grin broadly, float on. A pigeon coos. The time is not yet. A little longer the bare platform must wait by the empty kerb, till some stranger—a plump baldhead with hands thrust into pockets, vaguely discomfited by the challenge of Hair—pauses in the mid-distance to form an audience of one.

I have no desire to witness, and perhaps assist in, these manœuvres. In my temperament there's a good deal of Coleridge's Wedding Guest: I have to be on my guard against every skinny finger and gimlet eye. Suppose I found myself unsupported, caught up in painful arguments that left no way out to lunch, and my whole future compromised? It can't be risked. So, clutching at loud bassoons —in this instance the netball game—I hop away under the trees.

*   *   *   *

Than netball what could be more delightful? It might have originated with wastepaper-baskets behind one of those old solicitors' windows that look down on the square. Dickensian names like Mossop and Syms decorate doorways; high collars and high stools are brushed aside, and the young lady netballers come out to play. There they dance on the asphalt, defying nature by handling a round football and achieving such poses as the healthy young Englishman would start back from if it weren't sport.

The bandstand is empty: we revel in a music of Christian names, gasps, little shrieks of enjoyment or pain. And the sun flickers down on the hard curving walks and seat-ringed trees, the lawns of the Benchers' Garden nearby, the doors of the Soane Museum which will open as to a caller and divulge in circumstances of surrealist splendour Hogarth's 'Rake's Progress.'

From a sparrow-dotted space I look back. He—the weedy Samson who has cheated Delilah—has mounted his platform, and has a fair gathering. Laughter ripples across.

There's a budgerigar among the sparrows. It pecks at crumbs, fag-ends. Poor pretty thing, they exclaim, make a grab at it, and up it flies on a gilded branch.

*　　*　　*　　*

Of course, I'm holding off. I've known him for years; or rather he's been in the corner of my eye, that corner occupied by the itinerant and eccentric for whom London provides a stalking-ground. Emerging from station yards when everyone else rushes in; making his ascension on a moving staircase; slowly perambulating along Oxford Street in the dawn; on the steps of the British Museum, and looking up inquiringly at the bus marked 'Hackney Marsh Only'—yes, he must rank high among the semi-public figures. He has his meeting-places for different days of the week: Lincoln's Inn, Wednesday; City, Thursday ... On one of his Wednesdays was wafted to me, as I hurried by to lunch, the only word I have heard from him, uttered in tones of mild Cockney reproof: 'I'm not saying, madam, that I *am* Jesus Christ . . .' The remainder was lost, if there was (or could be) any remainder.

The dread of breaking *that* spell makes me kick my heels at one end of the Fields while he holds forth at the other.

*　　*　　*　　*

Well, I've made the mistake—if mistake it is—of listening. Transmigration of souls! You will never die! You have always lived!

'But, Mr. Owen,' objects one, 'if the number of spirits remain the same, how do you explain the fact that in the last hundred and fifty years the population of the world has more than doubled?'

There is, it seems, an explanation, involving branch or twin spirits, and the word 'eschatological'; and one of Mr. Owen's eyes grows other-worldly.

But this is deceptive. He attacks his attacker.

'You think you'll go to heaven?'

'Well——'

'Yes or no.'

'Yes—I hope.'

'Ha, but where is this heaven of yours—up there?'

'Suppose so.'

'But in Australia they say it's down *there*. No, my friend, heaven's not there or there, but here: we are all citizens of Heaven and don't know it . . . communion of spirits . . . extra-sensory impressions . . . '

'Where do you get all this, Mr. Owen?'

'By communing with my spirit.'

'Methylated!'

'Ah, you will have your little joke.'

He doesn't mind their little jokes, or an occasional shout of 'Gunga Din!' or 'Rasputin!'—which makes him slowly raise his thin arm to feel the biceps, in an attitude of prowess. His right eye strays to that non-existent heaven. There's a growl of thunder, which quite pleases him as though it were the wrath of some false god.

He complains of subjugation by the churches: they won't let him use their pulpits.

A newspaper—last week's *Times*—comes out of his pocket to provide texts for denunciation. O the wiles, the wickedness of money!

He prophesies. In ten years' time we shall all be Communist—but not the sort of Communist *we* mean—with abundance of trade, no Stock Exchanges, no tax-gatherers, no rent—

'No collection, Mr. Owen.'

None, he agrees, in that millennial epoch.

More imperative grows the thunder. Mr. Owen raises his fist, his voice—'We are dead and resurrected, immortal, eternal, and God is in each one of us . . .' Much of his eloquence is lost, carried to and fro on a rising wind.

'Flesh of flesh, life of life, spirit of spirit!'

Heavy raindrops fall, and out of nowhere a smart little bookie-man starts bustling round with a hat, into which all but the most stolid drop something.

Just in time! Crackle goes the thunder, down pours the rain, netball is abandoned, and we scatter for trees and doorways.

Only he is left. He sighs. He combs his dripping hair. He speaks to the two young policemen who with well-educated smiles have attended to every word. *The Times* is refolded. The platform is packed and shouldered. Serenely, across the storm-swept square, he resumes his journey through the ages.

Chelsea Militant

WE have left our mackintoshes, but uncertain remains the day, and London would be among the greyest sights on earth if it weren't for one thing. Look along Oxford Street; its buses have the colour I mean. Should everything splash (as it looks like doing), they will splash red. There's the pillar-box on the corner. Wait long enough, and you'll hear the exciting clang of a bell and see the yet more exciting fire engine race by.

London red seems to cling to the public offices, for besides transport, pillar-box, and fire-brigade, the sentries' coats are of the same hue, and veteran pensioners sport it down to the knee. Children's berets and gloves, women's tunics, idly pick out the theme along a crowded shop front. Oh, and there in a window-box—the very prototint of all this redness—is a geranium. Does it startle or soothe? Is it cheerful, angry, gay, repellent, dangerous, inviting, warming, beautiful, lively, or what? Who can say? In Spain it would advertise a bull-fight, in Rome a gathering of the faithful, in Moscow an armed rally. Here it means, if it means anything at all, people who don't see red.

But we do see—once in a year—a Flower Show, a Lord Mayor's procession, a Trooping of the Colour. Chelsea, you might say, is the Trooping of the Flowers. There they are in their full-dress uniform, the Rose Guards and the Tulip Regiment, the six-foot Delphiniums, the Sweet Pea Fusiliers, the Stocks, the plucky Irises, the Calceolarias and the Rhodies and Chrysanths, as well-drilled a force as ever you clapped eyes on. They've brought their bands with them, too. The instant we enter the marquee—Chelsea being now, except for the stalls and the gardens, one enormous marquee—the bands all strike up at once in discord, and somewhat shaken, but smiling our unconcern, we join the civilian party that crawls round to review the ranks.

How gorgeous they are, how brave, how they stare! What records, what medals! My own amazement (since I was never one for parades) gives way to adaptability, adaptability to critical haste, haste to despair, but a despair in which pleasure and cunning are beginning to assert themselves. Damn calceolarias! Grandeur and violence being the order of the day, I seek out what is delicate, seclusive, and small. The rock plants do not outstare or outsmart me; some of them—heaths, gentians, roses—are exquisite; I know of—let me see, now—an Iris, *Persica*, one to two inches high, with white, greenish blue, purple or orange flowers; this I require, and not finding, assume a much-needed superiority. Let Gloxinia threaten, lily sneer—I don't mind; and as I go round again (for always we must go round again, having missed 'something') I feel the strain of the occasion less. I meet, among the private exhibits of the Society, a fascia of vast overblown rhubarb stalks—that old emblem of gardening fatuity—and it revives my spirits.

But isn't it all—everybody is exclaiming—wonderful? Yes, almost too wonderful.

Although, perhaps, not *quite* as good as last year?

Well, perhaps not quite. But wonderful. And bigger and better blooms are promised for next year; so that, in the years to come, we may all be able to experience the tiptoe pride of the late King Victor Emmanuel inspecting his Palace Guards.

With a last flourish of brass, a chromatic cheer, a salute to marquee and prize garden, we are dawdling our way along the serpentine exit path that will be there long after the Flower Show is forgotten. One miserable flower accosts me; a plain, ordinary, twisty lupin rather dust-laden from the tramp of feet. How our glutted appetite scorns it; I avoid its eye, I pass it quickly, with the same uneasiness that will afflict me when I meet a beggar outside. But then I look back. The lupin, in all its disarray of pink spires and green cartwheel spokes, still trails appealingly over the path, and it has something I must have been looking for most of the afternoon. Yes, it's off duty. It doesn't strain. It's itself. Grandiflorescence hasn't even entered its head.

LOST!

WAITING for my bus and glancing along the shop fronts I meet the stare of Lost Property. It *is* a stare, quite unlike that 'shining, morning face' of the tobacconist's on one side, the grocer's on the other.

One's impression of an old-fashioned trunk stores is troubled by the variety of objects that have crept into the picture. Umbrellas, rugs, hand-bags—every niche filled; yet nothing, not so much as a galosh toe, allowed on the pavement. What has strayed once might be tempted again. But near by, roving the kerbs, will be found a prickly individual—himself the repository of wardrobes beyond restraint—with the placard 'Furs, Trunks, Suit-cases—Sale Now On.'

Out of the window, as out of a Snyders still-life, starts such an abundance, what with opera-glasses slung from accordions and the stoppered smile of a dressing-case supporting vanity-bags and billiard balls, that I am drawn forward in admiration; pyramids of almost new cases, shirts still in their transparent wrapping, barometers, made-up bow-ties (a whole corner devoted to these), socks, fancy and plain, velvet jackets, two Coronation coaches (the larger, pulled by eight horses, standing half a foot high), crystal wireless sets, squash rackets, shoe trees, sunshade clusters, a pair of skates volant—what detail! What *collectionism*!

Yet, unlike the still-life, it reflects not appetite but the lack of it. All these articles have been brought to their present exigency—for, despite a brave show, it's no less —by the simple fact of being not wanted. Abandoned! The accordion-player, leaving behind on the seat that instrument which had perhaps been the rallying point of a countryside, turned his back on light-fingered music; the telescope was laid down, not to resume its kindly surveillance of neighbours; typewriters mark the lapse into silence, and sextants a change of occupation. In the circumstances tragedy, which haunts the pawnshop's five coffee-spoons, is surprisingly absent.

Once, between the wars, I remember seeing a bird-cage.

Confidence wavers. Does railway travel encourage forgetfulness? Are there particular lines—those to Southend, for example, and Halifax—along which only the most resolute passengers, huddled behind drawn blinds and popped in and out of tunnels, will be able to fight off the choking fumes of amnesia? Till last week, introducing into the window a fine transverse sweep, there had been a pair of skis. Kilts, rubber dinghies one might bow the head to —but skis? How can anyone forget, lose, or let slip such a belonging? We must assume at once, I think, to keep our hold on solidities, a preternaturally good or bad skier. The first would have given rein to a sudden aversion, flinging them (after all, only his third-best pair) out of the carriage window, to try embankment slopes on their own.

I favour, however—after looking at it, at *them* from

many angles—the rash, silly performer. He—not she, I imagine—set out for Derbyshire with a week-end invitation. It was snowing: what more natural than to take skis? The fairyland of St. Pancras is left behind, the new Dornford Yates novel just peeped into—that must wait for the evenings; there's lunch among the white wastes of Nottingham, followed by a doze in the not-too-crowded carriage, and dreams of long, intertwining runs. He wakes with a jolt. What's happened? The sun is shining, the fields are green, barbarously the birds sing. He arrives in a midsummer haze to see his host—in flannels—standing to wave from a car: at this instant, to sundry bellowings and antics along the platform, his skis are unloaded. He cannot but disown them.

Still, that's only half the story. The skis, once abandoned, are never reclaimed. Why? The question will plague us with almost every article here except the most detestable or trivial. They can't all, the ex-owners, be rudely rich, or dead of a sudden, or behind bars. No, for a final explanation we must turn inwards, meeting there strange reluctances, wrong numbers, inquiries and applications, forms mislaid, months sliding away into the August rains with their call to the seaside. You know how it is!

What shadows now appear in the window! These gauntlets can never have brought warmth, these relinquished umbrellas preluded storm at home; the shiny new cases are, one and all, cases for Dr. Freud. A day may come when among these dread objects we shall recognize one, when—art thou there, truepenny?—the initials on the brief-case will be ours.

Meanwhile, possessively, somewhat sadly, I weigh the presence of certain objects—typewriters, for example, and Union Jacks—against the hardly less curious absence of others, including boots, books, hats, gloves, jewellery, watches. Where have they gone? What limbo attends buttons and pins?

Lost! Quite lost!

And I turn back for my bus; but it's away—lost!—and I must wait ten more minutes by this strangely inimical window.

Cornish Cream

'O R would you,' inquired Jim, the waiter, not without relish, 'prefer *semolina*?'

Some even did. Between seasons, with Easter behind and summer to come, the dining-room of the three-star hotel was almost empty. A refrigerator whirred and clacked in the distance, below lay the sea—the green-and-purple mobbing but not yet mobbed sea. On a lonely beach the long white lines curled, broke, drew back their sliding lace.

We watched, over our peach flan (what a peach, and what a flan!), the small diving bird that always diverted our lunch-hour and seemed to enjoy his. Not far off the bobbing lobster-pots providing a living larder; but what lobster had ever found its way to these tables? In August, we were assured by the waiter—whose deep tones rarely evaded the note of satire—on Sundays, lobster would be served.

But our very reason for making this first visit to Cornwall had been that, so far from August, we should find things quiet. Bluebells startled us under trees barely hinting green; in the high banks were violets and primroses, a rare ice-cream paper; the haze at sea and the mild blue overhead rounded our days. We took the car to grey churches in hollows. We walked on wet sand and discovered paper-weight worlds in the rocks. We listened to tales of sharkfishing, last winter's snow. We watched the boats go out and come back.

That very morning we had been filling in labels for tins of cream to be sent to friends.

'Won't you,' came the richly deceptive voice nearby, 'have some *more* semolina, madam?' (With the same solicitude he had hushed a new arrival with 'I hope you have enjoyed your dinner, sir.')

Would she? It wasn't possible. But the idea fascinated. She hesitated; regretfully, it seemed, shook her head. Another day, perhaps. Or if she had been a little younger... Over some of the meals only his wit and sympathy pointed a way. He had known other days, as a butler; in a famous grill-room; and was now, having sailed through the driving test, ready to qualify as the perfect chauffeur. We wished him luck, dollars.

He was, of course, a Cornishman, which the hotelier was not, and in this part of the world never is. One evening, as with delicacy he set before us the processed peas, he got talking about the pub on the quay, cider, summer evenings, and one Old Willow, a lanky ancient who peddled his ferry-boat (when he felt like it) and at night lit up the 'Merry Mariners,' conspicuous from the yellow waistcoat bequeathed by a visitor. 'Goes home by rail every night,' said our *famulus*, vanishing through swing-doors. We were still weighing this when he returned with 'Feeling his way across the bridge, you know, full of scrumpy.' Scrumpy is the rough cider, three or four pints of which, at 1o*d*. a pint, will render jelly-kneed the most stalwart. Two before dinner one evening I had found more than enough; though when it came to dinner I was glad.

Then we poked into corners pretty thoroughly. One day we'd pack off to a Furry Dance, another would confront us with Wesley, laying stones here, greeted with them there; our car acquired new scratches ('Look out for the natives' arrows'). When it blew an Atlantic gale we hugged the Channel, and a sou'wester would drive us north. The pyramidal heights about St. Austell and ghost mines of Redruth formed a watershed from which we would choose weathers; and one afternoon following the white rush of a china-clay stream we came on an amazing sight through the V of the downs: the whole bay tinctured with the greens and blues of kaolin. To digest the whole we popped into one of the 'Cream Teas' cottages with a verandah and gobbled up a piled plate of scones, butter, cream, and jam.

Little lanes led to coves. Mousehole was less spoilt than Polperro, a veritable museum of piskified attractions; Portloe than either. But someone had got there first: a crafty innkeeper who had snapped up the local pub and turned it into a Dispense, introduced art in a thousand delectable and dubious forms, put flower names on the bedrooms and set the electric logs twinkling. The fishermen got their own back by clattering in the dawn and hanging stinking bait about the rocks under his windows.

When we did find the perfect cove—which shall remain nameless—it looked as unreal as a stage scene. The rocks that had so often found their way on to canvas seemed themselves painted; gulls had been laid on by television; fussy, inactive fishermen were only doing a bit of business between the verses of grand opera.

· After that we saw artiness, camouflage, invasion everywhere. Shopkeepers, daubers and knitters, landladies were waiting behind every curtain; more and more we were haunted by the ghost legions to follow, sucking ices, chewing chips, dipping piskies in wells, and introducing to the mole and the wren the Light Programme. Flying saucers had been seen, in good time for Whitsun. Of course, we ought to have waited and gone with the swim. What finally shot us out of Cornwall altogether—with only mild regrets for its bleak devastated charm—was the board 'Bed and Breakfast' staked on a fresh-dug plot, the house not yet half built.

But before going on into Devon—which, incidentally, we found more congenial—we went back to our original seaside, and stayed a night at the hotel next to that we had started from. We remembered a saying of the *famulus*, that his favourite reading was the menu next door; and, for once, lobster met us on the plate.

As the lights wriggled down into the harbour we glanced across at the 'Merry Mariners.' A figure emerged, paused. Old Willow? No. Jim himself, on his night off; going home by rail, full of scrumpy.

WHEN for the sixth time the games-mistress comes running round the summer-house, to halt, cry 'Girls! Girls!' flaunt distress, and unconcernedly join the band of those she seeks everywhere, it may seem more than a case of end-of-term nerves. Obsession has us all in its grip. Consultations. Awkward interval. Then off again, poor lady—with what high hopes that this time will mend everything—in obedience to her strange compulsion.

The sun shines. Trees dream. In the silence one can hear leaves stirring, and that pad-pad-pad behind the summer-house, coming instantly nearer . . . disquieting, but for the fact that it's Miss Joyce Grenfell, caught in the rut of film-making.

Work wouldn't be going smoothly without this occupational stutter which to an outsider gives every film work in progress its resemblance to a page by Gertrude Stein.

What makes it more oddly, frantically appealing is that the moment so suspended, going round and round for

ever, is—was, or will be—a particle of fun from St.
Trinian's. Most of us know St. Trinian's already, and
that's why it's being filmed. The joke that exploded in
the fiendish 'forties, imprinting on the mind its sudden
lethal shadows, has proved radio-active. Those girls
annihilated us, and went. Regulation blue seemed a little
less black. When we had still to jump off the pavement
to let a trio of them pass we felt only a twinge of old
nightmare and returned to the comforts of Sophie
Tuckshop, Bessie Bunter, and Mr. Arthur Marshall's
dispatches from the cocoa front. It is said that Searle
himself, slyly responsible for the whole thing, slammed
the door on St. Trinian's before taking new steps into
seriousness and rum. All over . . . But here, gym-suited,
arms and legs flying, with the appeal 'Call me sausage'
never far absent, comes Miss Grenfell again.

This time success welcomes her. She is given a short
break before some new punishment ('Stand by the goal-post
and say fifteen times "I won't nark it" ') descends on her.
I have been well primed with synopsis, notes on the cast,
and even a St. Trinian's Magazine hazy from the press, so
that when we snatch a few words I know I am addressing a
policewoman disguised as a games-mistress.

Miss Grenfell is an aspiration, an educational system in
herself, but belonging to the Marshall rather than the
Searle School. However, when the screen sets out to net
a joke it hauls in all sorts of neighbouring jokes, big and
small. Here, besides funny policewomen, will be found
the funny civil servant; his role in films is to take over
leaky or haunted mansions, billet boys' schools on girls',
and go native in wild surroundings. Within this very
summer-house—a grimly Gothic affair—which has been
Miss Grenfell's mulberry bush, live two of them; they

came down investigating; soon they will be joined by a third.

Then as the headmistress there's that ruby among comedians, who could induce a soft plausibility anywhere, Mr. Alastair Sim. He is far from being—it's impressed on me—the pantomime dame. Changes of sex are in the air and the stills hold a promise of baroque splendour, over which, when a reiteration of events grows tedious, I may ponder. Yet however strict may be Mr. Sim's performance, it must be added to those auxiliary jokes mentioned. He's not here in person. They finished shooting him on Monday.

Not the girls—no, *not* the girls, though there was a time when they would have romped to it. Do you remember 'Girls, girls, a little less noise, please,' as the machine-gun stuttered into the cloister and a shocked headmistress, not Mr. Sim, popped her head out? And that same figure —I think it was the same—dangling limp from a tree while with delighted gurgles her four assassins below nod to one another, 'O.K.—now for old Stinks'? That marked, I think, the end of St. Trinian's. They had smoked during prayers, burnt down the east wing, roasted an ox, drawn the cork from the gin bottle: they could do no more.

Except, of course, with an oath, go on the films. But having got there, what a transformation awaits them! High heels, black silk stockings, protuberant yellow sweaters, tights, hair lights, eye shadow, all for the match against St. Helen's—and perhaps a little for you and me.

'No,' says the director thoughtfully, when with a startled appreciation of this hockey eleven I have inquired about broken limbs, 'no murder. But'—and he brightens a little—'one of our sixth-formers is *married*.'

This atrocity seems to unite everything, the unreal summer-house, the sunlit lawn with its groupings of rubber-booted mechanics and made-up faces, the moor-hens skipping over lily pads (and having nothing to do with it), the old red-brick manor in the distance over-awed by concrete sheds and offices. And surely the sixth form, with their marl and cream complexions, must that very morning have burst into front-page adolescence.

True, in the fourth form, perched about a trolley of some sort, there are wrinkled stockings, manes of hair, waggled branches, and here and there a wild odd look that may promise to threaten east wings. A matronly lady knits over them, and as little film actresses expecting two or three pounds a day they earn it kicking their heels.

Miss Grenfell and some of the big ones move up for action. An arc-light blanches the sunlit faces. The camera peers, and sound leans a long arm over. There are re-hearsals, more rehearsals, takes. It's like charades. A little man darts forward to powder Miss Grenfell's nose. Hush, comes the word. Our conversations are reduced to whis-pers and we go—go finally—on tiptoe.

It has been odd and fascinating and irksome, and I'm sure that what comes of it will be fun, because Mr. Frank Launder, the sad man in the overcoat chiefly responsible, has already brought off that gallivant you probably remember, *The Happiest Days of Your Life*.

Our car has to be back in Piccadilly at five; it's not ours, but a large stranger that knows the way blindfold and will be saluted by the gate-man as we turn out of what looks like an Atomic Research station. Under Constabulary skies we take the flat, flat road. A bicyclist ducks, hoping to see stars. My thoughts are wrapped in the new St. Trinian's. Is it hockey? Does it Searle? Will scholasticism still shake its head over the reflection that girls, at St. Trinian's anyway, will be ghouls?

Elegant Pub

AT first I thought I'd made a mistake, and was turning to go, when the lady in the white coat smiled, and I smiled and said 'Pint of bitter, please,' and she urged 'Best bitter?' and best bitter it was. Still I doubted my eyes. Gold-dusted ceiling, claret wallpapers of an exclusive design, crimson-foliaged plants, table mats on tip-toe tables—such a rare, such an elegant pub!

I'd stepped in from one of London's multifarious high streets whither, on a day of confused duty, the zigzag had led. That morning I had set out in search of (be frank) a female newt. I already had a male newt which incautiously I had shown to a small boy, who required a pair for his birthday—tomorrow. So, in spare moments, I made various telephone calls and bus journeys, to find at last in a Kilburn pet stores what I demanded: one newt, female.

Mark the qualification. Camden Town could offer me schools of newts, all male; male also had been the newt population of Walthamstow, Stoke Newington, Dulwich. At Kilburn they hadn't been sure, they'd see—would I hold on? The tidings came that they had just one. Keep it, I exclaimed, I'll be along.

And there, held up by the tail for approval, had been

this rare female, price sixpence. Very good, I said. A moistening of water in the bottom of the jar would, I was assured, keep her happy.

It was a warm day, and twenty past five; that parched moment between afternoon and evening, shop-shut and pub-tide, as delicately poised as the jam jar now masked in a paper bag.

I dawdled along the shop-fronts enjoying not only the windows but the uses they make of language: here were snips and stockists, hearty cabbages and fresh cues, a handsome manliness (it was claimed) of sandals, sincere tailoring, hygienic bakery. How expressive the epithet—sincere, for example, as applied to cloth and thread; it conjured up the tailor himself working till all hours and caring for every stitch, unlike those who skimp seams for the sake of wide shoulders. The other tailoring term is, more mysteriously, bespoke.

Then there's the fulsomeness of those grief-stricken places where the word is sacrifice, and slashed prices vie with astounding bargains and unrepeatable offers. Next, the butcher, a man of plain speech. No kind hearts decorate his window, no pure tripe, or splendid chaps. For him suet is suet, offal offal: even 'prime'—that one noble, butcherly affix—has vanished. Yet to what heights of language will he not reach, even announcing himself, outside Victoria station, as 'De Ath, Family Butcher'? . . .

At that moment the pub opened.

So there I was, swallowing my pint, in the very latest of pubs, in N.W.6.

Not only wallpapers and furniture but embellished sky-lighting and a bar all mirrors with every reflected bottle in place and a glimpse of *collage* and a botanical-nautical screen and an air-blue dining-room in the distance brought

associations remote from the idea 'saloon.' Was this indeed
'The Cock' in Kilburn and not, say, a landing of the
Festival Hall, or a ballet designed by Mr. Cecil Beaton?
Could I just sit there, drinking best bitter, and reading
about murders and cricket, and wanting—if the truth
must be told—to take a look in my paper bag?

This impulse so much got the better of me that I walked
(or miserably shuffled) out through the glassy vestibule and
round into the public where, if the walls weren't quite
decided, the atmosphere was easier. Four men and a fat
woman sat under a dart-board, which was there, I suspect,
because it presented a valid shape.

I peeped into my jar: how young and charming she was
in her new leaf green, with a guinea-fowl-feather tail,
delicate legs, long fingers, goldy eyes that regarded me out
of black centres: prettier even than the scene I'd just
quitted.

'Female newt,' I remarked to the others, who nodded
and went on with their game of distantly pulling the
barman's leg.

Awful notices frowned on us: no Music, Dancing, or
Singing; no Betting or Gambling in any form; and no
Swearing or Obscene Language. What price the new look!

Now a new London pub is like a new meerschaum: it
must colour up, and I wondered how, with smoke inside
and fog out, this one would do that.

My last glimpse, after I'd crossed the street holding my
paper bag in front, was of lustrous lobby and date boasted
in stone; first licensed 1486. In five centuries the house
must have known many changes. Now it emerges, from
the drawing-board of Mr. Geoffrey Crockett, as an
elegant pub. Or should I say, the pub elegant? For not
only the adjective, but its placing, may prop or let down.

Dead End

IT was getting dusk, and the lamps had been lit in the main thoroughfares, but not here. Two straight little rows, each a drabber reflection of the other; invisible trains passing; the high brick wall at the end. Under that wall, but along one pavement only, a small crowd staring across. I walked slowly along to join them, having first made sure of my destination—Rillington Place.

Rillington Place—you may frown—surely that name seems familiar? Indeed it does! All through one April week-end it was inescapable. No matter where in the British Isles you lived, or what the tinge of your newspaper, from Printing House Square grey to Bouverie Street yellow, it will have found you out: 10 Rillington Place was the address of the 'Notting Hill Murders.' For

Londoners, during a week-end solemnized by the lying-in-state of Queen Mary, it acquired suddenly a hideous, an exorbitant interest as day after day, and then almost hour by hour, the placards screamed their three and four victims . . . . five! . . . six! . . . possibly seven! A certain stoicism in the matter began to assert itself.

> Any man has to, needs to, wants to
> Once in a lifetime, do a girl in—

as, with characteristic moderation, Mr. T. S. Eliot has put the matter. However, if at Rillington Place the assassin could work prodigies, so also could the police. By day and by night boardings had been ripped down, walls and floors flayed, and the search extended to a garden which (one might be forgiven for supposing) could scarcely have served any other purpose. Speculation soared; vans came and went. Sunday brought such an influx of strollers, sight-seers with sandwiches in their pockets, and habitual crowd-swellers, that the street had to be cleared and barriers erected.

All these had vanished when, on the Monday evening, I resorted that way. It had taken some finding, being (despite the reporters) nowhere on Notting Hill, but in a remote depression of North Kensington, where chap-fallen streets are the rule and the palings before some of the houses enclose little more than a dustbin clump. Shops had shut; pubs were open to their regular half-dozen; a few people were hurrying home or loitering out daylight under a lamp-post. I passed two West Indians with strange gaieties of shirt peeping out from raincoats, a nun in full sail, before turning into the quiet—which developed into a hush—of Rillington Place.

The *other* pavement was stark empty: a machine-gun

might have been set up on the corner. The last house abutting the wall was No. 10, five-windowed, two-storeyed, with an ugly bow-front next the door, like the others. What distinguished it was the almost sealed look of its patched curtains, this giving the only hint of activities within. The building, small as it was, had housed several tenants, now of course evacuated. Such confinement might, understandably, breed thoughts of murder—but its accomplishment? How establish a murderous habit? Yet presumably it had been done. And the knowledge coloured, or discoloured, the view. Already No. 10 had an ugly pathos, that much-photographed look which will appeal to future 'students of crime'—that is to everyone. If the perfect murder—that ideal so often dreamed of by lofty souls—is the murder perfectly domiciled and landscaped, then here surely it was. The very door cracks, a certain shininess where the paint had rubbed off, proclaimed it: hieroglyphs, if ever there were such, of evil.

But at this moment, out of the window of No. 9, stepped a man. He wasted no time, but set about cleaning his windows. How his rag whirled! What polishings and squeakings! We attended breathlessly. No possibility of his falling: a couple of feet below was the bow roof. But the awfulness of his side of the street had been snapped. His actions, as negligently he swayed this way and that, announced that *he* had nothing to hide, *his* windows weren't afraid to let the light in, whatever might be going on next door.

We relaxed a little; the women's heads (mostly they were women) leant together; children skipped; a train passed, rumbling away over a bridge. There was some conversation in which gardens, Easter, vans, the Two

E

Thousand Guineas, and the price of cauliflowers mingled not incongruously.

Then very slowly the door—*the* door—began to open. From the crowd, instantly alert, came a gasp, a slight pressing forward. A dog barked. The door hesitated; and having opened a foot or so, as slowly closed again.

A little dog—whose, they wondered?—ran right out into the street, yapped furiously, lost heart, and sidled away.

Again the door was opening, this time a little wider, to extrude the head and shoulders of a policeman; such a very young, fair policeman, helmeted, who with hasty unconcern looked at nothing—and especially not at us—and withdrew. Someone might have said to him 'Pop your head out.' So had he done.

Thereafter No. 10 kept itself to itself: Downing Street couldn't have been more seclusive, more decorously mobbed. I wish I could convey the inevitability with which the whole scene and the proceedings (or lack of them) were imbued. There is a cycle of retribution so well established—investigation, hue-and-cry, arrest, judgment —that it's almost as though an act sprung from the people had gone back to them, to be assessed with a verdict from twelve good men and true. No less good and true, I'm convinced, were the twenty-four women upstanding here: Ladbroke women after a classical pattern.

With night coming on I quitted them, having swelled the chorus by one, and now leaving them as I'd found them. It occurred to me with a glance back that, like many another imprisoning alley, Rillington Place would be hung and cross-hung with flags for a Coronation in June.

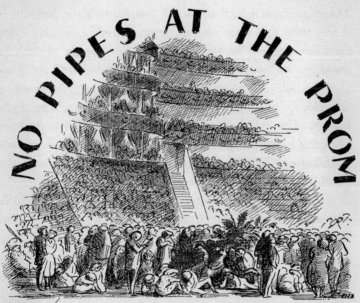

NO PIPES AT THE PROM

HE Proms—or to give them their full title, the Henry Wood Promenade Concerts—are in the thick of a Diamond Jubilee. Shall we go along? A pleasant buzz, a to-and-fro about that old beehive the Albert Hall, makes us quicken our pace. (How elegant, these days, is the Memorial with its cross-hatch of scaffolding!)

The worry is not about getting in but where to get in, and where to go next. So many levels attract, such corridors circling before and behind, that have known boxers and Hiawathans, the tramp of the W.V.S., the assurance 'Millions now living will never die.' A scatter of applause starts us running. Of course, it may be only the first violin . . .

One pays most to sit nearest those who stand: their endurance, as of Christians in the arena, unflinching, pale, flushed, lapsed about a fountain, dreadfully heartens us. There are goldfish, too, in the fountain. Then behind, in three tiers, rise the boxes from which one can comfortably see and be seen; over these—highly serious, if tempting to programme-droppers—the balcony, whither I am bound; and round and above all, a top promenade or triforium, night-blue through its arches, where Echo haunts. The whole bursts on me together with Brahms' 'Tragic Overture.'

Being only just in time, like a late arrival for a photographic group, I fall at once into the general catalepsy. No dappled deer in a shade or burglar by moonlight could be stiller; I daren't move, smile, or sigh; I seem quite under the spell. But why, when I chance a Prom, must it always be Brahms? That magician has a loose grip. He brings the most wonderful gift and keeps losing it in armfuls, in oceans, of brown paper. Crackle, crackle.

Inside my armour, between a rapture and a yawn, I'm beginning to wake up. Can't help myself. One toe ventures a beat. Stop it! Another pulses. Out of the rigid countenance (what, by the way, is that fly doing there?) the eyes start exploring like mice. At first they play about near home, down a trouser-crease, over the bald head in front, across someone's programme notes, and along the balcony rail.

With a dive they're off: *I'm* off, however much I may dissociate myself from such bat-wings or skylarking.

Joyously I hover, circle, and swoop. I peep into boxes where pink-and-white schoolgirls are packed like fondants or a frail Indian shrinks (so it seems) from a glistening butcher; I occupy the seat next a vision in rose; I ring round the angry score-reader and the yet angrier protester behind who hisses as each page is swept over; I pass Lady Macbeths in picture hats about to set off sleep-walking, a bride at the window, a thin-haired clerk at the end of a row turned away as *Le Penseur*.

But that's only the beginning. During the Third Symphony we all have space—with little chirps and squeaks which the listener at home may put down to atmospherics—to reconnoitre our waxwork ranks, explore the crimson-and-gilt East and the pale Wedgwood West, perch about the great organ, chase flying notes round the roof, whisper indelicacies to the black-coated attendant with folded hands, press our noses against the B.B.C.'s glass compartment, and even airily throng, as on a *Punch* cover, the London Symphony Orchestra.

A dinner-jacket may not seem the ideal costume for the parts they have to play, these actors of a passion by turns moody and tripping, but it has become as much part of music as the notes on the score. Brass is a bold fellow; wood-wind blows over sheep on a hillside or charms snakes; the fiddler cradles a babe, plucks at our heart-strings; double-basses initiate a donkey Derby; and at the back, with his goods on show, is our ironmonger.

Brahms has only one ironmonger; but after the interval modernism will contrive a row of ironmongers, all rising together, a heaven of harps, rallies of horns, bells, harness, and who knows what else. Stravinsky once thought of introducing scent-sprays, just the thing for a Prom, though their deployment might be difficult.

This evening there are no singers. Pity; they can add so much, especially during their long wait; six or seven of them, and one little chap who seems to sit on. How our hearts go out to him! He *should* sit on, and then at the end get up and bow with the others.

But back to Brahms: the vanloads of brown paper are joyously flung about, dived into, up comes the jewel, off it goes again, and in a perfect whirl of wrappings the Third ends.

Bravo! Bravo!

Those in the arena have shouted it for us. We clap, a little longer than need be. Interval and the bar, where nearly everyone crowds to talk excitedly and drink tea.

For the second half I go Promming. Martyrdom has taken its toll, and quite half of those left are seated on the floor or reclining: students on holiday and workers out of shops and offices, as many girls as men. A few seem to be starting on walking tours. But no beards, no bravado, and no tobacco haze.

I miss the pipes. Pipes are as necessary to a Prom as to Pan. Before the war everyone used to smoke furiously, especially for Wagner, and between movements there was a regular *feu d'artifice* of the indomitables lighting up and puffing away. Not to join in was to label oneself no promenader. But now I see one pipe, which its owner makes no attempt to smoke but sucks meditatively.

Here, we are under the very shadow of music (a rather pale, pretty concerto by Alan Rawsthorne) and of the baton—*our* conductor. He plays Rawsthorne, but even more Hamlet or Solness with his back to us. Through the inexpressiveness of tails he must transmit abandon and delicacy, longings never satisfied, a pride often wounded to the quick; he must fly into transports and rages, lean over a brink, plunge, hack, stab, snatch in a strayed bassoon (out of his surreptitious study, it may be, of space fiction), summon a drum-beat from the dead, put out all sound. Henry Wood, whose effigy now looks over us, was a master of the *pianissimo*: with his baton he would make everything recede to a mere gnat-sound, his finger would be raised to his lips, his shoulders would hunch, and stricken, shaking his head and resisting the air, he would step back in a very ecstasy of dismay. His sweats horrified; the carnation saved. He was the Fourth B in person. The only protagonist of his stature to appear in the present season is Sir Thomas Beecham, making a first ambassadorial bow to Prom audiences.

Reeling, I wander off through the Park, where music would look and feel better, and where the Memorial scaffolding, I notice, rises to a height of ten feet above its monument. Can they mean to add something? The leaves sigh—a small bird darts across the water—I find myself humming. . . . Brahms.

A Plea for the Bronze and Stone Men

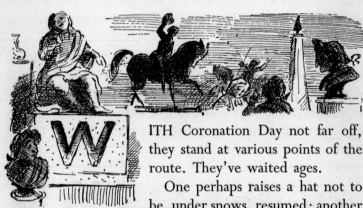

WITH Coronation Day not far off, they stand at various points of the route. They've waited ages.

One perhaps raises a hat not to be, under snows, resumed; another takes towards his old headquarters or club a first step that's also the last; a third struggles to cry 'Halt!' and multitudinously the traffic sweeps on. How illustrious they are, but how dull, these personages of yesterday!

Hard things have been said about them, as that they got more—or no more—than they deserved. Our grandfathers heaped honours: we grudge the one honour remaining—a glance. Or if we do, in passing, glance up, it is to resent looks so unappetizing, an eminence grown turgid. Fashions change, oratories stiffen. Never a *new* battle or policy to harp on! There's nothing like immortality for reducing a man.

On the whole the Generals and the Admirals come off

best. A certain alacrity belongs to the hand on the sword-hilt or (in favoured cases) loosely handling reins: life has taught them, if nothing else, to seem ready aye ready, and the experience serves well. They scan horizons, ignore defeat, and expose themselves—and others—unflinchingly. Of course we haven't the faintest idea who they are; but this may spur curiosity. Also they may—*must*—wear hats of a striking oddity.

No such alleviation either of headgear or temperament is allowed the Politician (statesman should he be called?), who may even have been summoned, as to a snap division, in his bath robe. Thus Canning; but not, one is thankful to say, Disraeli; who might have taken such usage hardly. Yet the one as the other evidences that plasticity without which there would be no appeals and no dissolutions, no running on the rocks, no forced marches in promised lands. The country's ruin has passed safely to others' keeping. Yet how the gesture must still ominously cajole, how the outstretched hand must kindle a torch and nab a vote! It's not the easiest of attitudes to sustain, and no wonder a few look tired. In none, however, has weakness so far triumphed as to suggest the possibility of being *found out*.

That indignity is reserved for the simpletons—mostly poets—who have been relegated to odd corners. One look at Shakespeare, dawdling in Leicester Square and propping himself on a misquotation from his works, should be enough to convince anyone that they were written by Major-General Berry. What he is also doing in Westminster Abbey, cheek by jowl with the Duke of Argyll and Adam Lindsay Gordon, heaven or Apollo alone knows.

The Generals (and Admirals) and the Politicals are in command of the Trafalgar and Parliament Square areas respectively: the West End ones, that's to say, for lone leaders may be encountered as far afield as Bow Road and Greenwich Park. The two juntas don't, either geographically or in style, infringe on one another; and both, of course, are splendidly situated for the Coronation procession in its great wheeling movements.

But having waited so long, will they even see it? For some the answer is already decisive. As the stands have gone up, so also has the boarding round fame; first the plinth, then the legs disappear; until at last—as in a Turkish bath cabinet—only the head remains. Poor towelled Canning! But worse follows. After an interruption, during which the stand canopy has been added, builders approach with a few planks and a lid, which— leaving no time for motions or petitions—they clap on.

So, already boxed, is Palmerston; Derby and Peel, having addressed the empty benches for weeks, will soon follow; Lincoln rises from his chair protesting. Of what avail now, Disraeli may be wondering, to have trod primrose paths! It seems monstrous, this banishment without reason or appeal—imposed, be it said, irrespective of party—the more so as, on the Parliament side, Cromwell stays. True, almost dislodged by benches, he will get a poor view of it all, but that he would take anyway.

And the Generals and the Admirals (it would need a special grant to eclipse Nelson) have escaped even so much as a finger laid on them!—Is this fair? Haven't they done their worst too? It may be, of course, that a series of last minute raids has been planned; that, man and horse, they will vanish in a surprise attack—themselves unsurprised— on the very eve. Let us hope so; or there will be murmurings that better strings can be pulled at the uniformed than at the black-coat end of Whitehall.

Others, under eaves and in alcoves are presumably

138

raised above controversy. The Home Office can boast a distinguished gathering of Lands, Pursuits, Sciences, Crafts, and Arts, who will bring their high seriousness to bear on the occasion. There they sit or recline; in one hand is posed a melon, compasses, writing tablets; the left breast (but how irreproachably) remains bare. If in the heat of the day horseplay should develop anywhere, it won't be, we may assure ourselves, here. None of Mr. Epstein's anthropoids has succeeded, I think, in climbing to a vantage point on the actual route, though the possibility should not be overlooked.

But there are—let us not relax vigilance—within sight of Parliament and Abbey, by the dozen and the score, huge, shaggy, indefinable male creatures whose heads struggle out of stone itself! Who or what they are, these savagely immured beings of the Treasury, how they got there, what their hopes and intentions, could hardly be guessed. Their looks, as they thrust through port-holes or between floors, we may appraise for ourselves—sad, unbridled, with locks cascading, manes rioting into beards, eagle's-wing moustaches; one moustache (on the corner of King Charles Street) even being woven—horrible fancy!—into two long pigtails or plaits. Here are dogfish in the hair, storm-tossed vessels. Oceanic is the threat; and although, as yet, imprisoned to the neck, these natures seem quite other than those fatherly ones similarly left buried in Margate sands. Are they reliable? We may well ask. I think here the Provost Marshal's office have certainly a case for screening, political or actual.

However, the Day will come (and let's hope it's a fine one), controversy will have been laid aside, and one thing is certain: nobody will grudge Charles I his privilege of the best view in London.

Oh, Jolly 3-D!

OF course, we all insisted we wouldn't go, but there we were: some frankly excited, others holding aloof, a few remembering their first talkie with Al Jolson imploring the skies, and a very few that Edwardian dark-room at the end of a pier in which, while one enjoyed, say, a vision of rough seas, the theatre itself rolled and pitched. Great days, when custard-pies *were* custard-pies, and any bicycles without riders would make straight for, and through, the nearest china-shop.

But already the news—stale news from a flat world—was over, and the lights were up. We looked round. Distinguished strangers present: hurriedly we felt for our own spectacles, tried them on, blinked, dandled.

FOR YOUR FURTHER ENJOYMENT

came the beauteous lantern-slide on the screen,

OUR STAFF WILL NOW VISIT ALL PARTS OF THIS THEATRE

(that meant poor fat Annie—charladying days over—with her tray).

PLEASE KEEP TO YOUR SEATS

(which, with Annie, seemed not difficult).

So, sucking the ice-creams which represent, we are told, the sole source of profits to impoverished British film-mongers, we cooled our rising excitement.

140

Spectacles on! In the confusion old Dr. Crunchbones had his, I swear, upside down, so that probably he'd see everything hollow; but then he always had. Miss Tripp, smiling, had pocketed hers. To a roar of music the title flashed up, *Thick Men*; it didn't merely flash, it floated; behind, with a mileage that made us suddenly feel our seats had been pulled from under us, was a man—a thick man—poised on parapet, who slowly leant forward and disappeared, leaving the recession of river, quay, sky-scraper, and sunset, into which we might all have disap-peared if the foreground titles hadn't, like a sort of in-flamed masonry, held us back. We were discovering who had played the banjo, and who fiddled the hair-do's, when the splash from below hit us.

The film itself—but how can one hope to imprint such things? Enough that this one was well up, or down, to standard, having taken advantage of 3-D to get back to the heart of things: the heroine (rather charmingly 3-D, I thought) chewed gum and drawled 'Oh, yeah?' and the hero, always getting into fixes and out of them, would stop short to exclaim 'Let's go' or 'You can't do this to me'; nor could they; ropes and writs wouldn't hold him; for seven reels—here's the moral—you may get away with murder, but the eighth will find you out, probably on top of Chicago's highest skyscraper. He had an engaging habit, this swell guy, of blowing smoke-rings over us. For 3-D, you must know, works forwards as well as backwards. Half the time they were sticking out elbows over the stalls or reclining their feet on the circle, and when the whole mob pulled guns you were fortunate if the muzzles nudged past you to someone else's waistcoat behind. This —with some relief—brought the first interlude.

And there we were, looking like Sunday afternoon on

141

the Brighton front, and remarking 'Wonderful,' 'Better than grandpa's stereoscope,' 'But when they move at all quickly they seem to go off—kind of crinkly,' 'Just as well, I couldn't stand much more.'

Resuming, we were double-crossed, followed and frisked, run over, dangled from heights, swept to the wail of police sirens through satiny night, plunged into the glory of a night-club—the thick man's (and woman's) hide-out. Cops were there too; thicker and thicker; not even they knew one from t'other. We watched from the little high grille in the boss's office. He was getting that eighth-reel feeling; the heights were calling. 'Let's go,' a farewell to his lady—her lips protruding, filling the theatre like hippopotamus lips—second interlude.

'Phew!' 'She loves him, though, doesn't she?' 'What good's that, his best friend's a cop, see?' 'Colour a bit patchy.' 'Oh, well, can't expect everything.'

Off again. Bang-bang. He must climb seventy-six floors, and the lift out of order. With that cop close behind. 'My pal,' he snarls over his shoulder, as he leaps for the fire-escape.

There's a scream. 'He's pinched my spectacles, the beast!' 'What?' 'Liar!' 'Who?' 'Give 'em back!' 'Let go!' 'Swine!' 'I'll inform the management!' And in less than no time, followed by more bang-bangs, we were all out in the street shouting, struggling.

Well I wonder. These thick men—who in their time have been jittery, silent men, and then sleek yap-yap or sing-song men, and sometimes, amazingly, rainbow men whisked from beef-red to cheese-green in a trice—I don't quite know how they're going to take to their new freedom. Suppose, during a matinée—it's been a long while coming—one of them were simply to *walk off the screen*? Would the rest follow? Should we have fugitive Neros, Henry ploughing through the stalls after Anne Boleyn, stampedes from chain-gangs, Carthage, the *Titanic*? Will there be an end to the Civil War, both sides deserting? It remains to be seen; if need be, resisted. 3-D has come to the local.

Shaw's Corner—Any Offers?

T O LET notices had brought us out on this rather chill afternoon, chasing and chased along A600. Past Hatfield we sliced; we shaved Welwyn. Getting warmer! (But it didn't feel so.) There through the trees was the Garden City, old as Garden Cities go, where Shaw lodged before settling at Ayot St. Lawrence.

The signpost pointed left into country neither hilly nor flat, open nor wooded. We had the lanes to ourselves. Was it here pilgrims had flocked—walked, biked—to catch a glimpse of the old Knickerbocker Glory? Not a ting, not a tyre-mark? After all that brag and gab—

nothing? Hedges and trees seemed to have returned to themselves.

Then a couple of fields off rose a Greek temple, some landlord's whim—admired by a few—to oust the existing church, which abides decently in ruins; and we came to a bend and the second and greater folly: Shaw's Corner.

The proprietary gate, lettered in iron, barred a New Rectory, far newer than the temple, and ugly and assertive into the bargain. Shaw paid £6,000 for it. You might wonder why.

You might wonder why the bulk of his fortune was left to the cause of phonetic spelling, a little to the drama, nothing at all to the upkeep of this mansion for which, after the failure of an appeal fund to raise more than a few hundreds, the National Trust now seeks a tenant. Only £170 per annum is asked, and the lessee—should such eventuate—will find himself with a roomy house, an acre of ground, his own power plant and car park, and the obligation at week-ends to fling open to the trail of feet and eyes Shaw's study.

We stood in the hall. The just-as-it-was look halted us (my wife remarking 'What a cold house!'), drew the eye to a piano with the lid raised and Schubert's songs. Here, when Mrs. Shaw was ill upstairs, he would sit playing and singing opera (early Italian, not Wagner), and air-raids— not very frequent, one imagines—provided the background for Mozart. Tableau. Mrs. Pat Campbell turns up with the caption when in one of her letters she begs him not to send photographs, which will only be given away, though she has rather fancied 'the one of you as Jesus Christ playing the piano.' Mrs. Pat! Ellen Terry! How wickedly warm they are, and how much in love with love he, like any Elizabethan sonneteer!

But further? Having been dazzled, and never having been able to find real Shaw, I suppose I was looking for him here, in the beautiful Chinese pigeon over the closed stove; more prints of birds up the stairs wall. A fowl himself, of the capering sort? Ah, the hat-stand! But a big colonial hat told nothing except that he liked playing the stranger. Sticks and canes—a confusion——

The caretaker's wife, quietly appearing, handed us a very thin polished cane in the head of which was a tiny flash-bulb. He liked toys, and hated twilight.

We were led to the study. This, then, was to be the museum piece. But when had it not looked famous? Shelved on two sides with reference books, histories, editions of Shaw; window desk and typewriter, shrouded; caricatures crowding the fire nook; filing cabinets.

'Thirty-six of 'em,' said the caretaker who had joined us, 'empty now.'

So we stared at the cabinets and at drawers of envelopes in which once had been snapshots. Gene Tunney's name came up; a most orderly tool-box was exhibited, a package addressed only with a sketch of Shaw and the words 'wherever he may be.' But that was the whole point: Where, ever, *was* he? Not in this den, with its Shaw trophies everywhere, as photographic as the Sherlock Holmes room seen a few years ago.

More Shaws in the drawing-room including Rodin's, and for the first time, crowning the mantelpiece, Charlotte Shaw. That marriage of the Shavian Phœnix and Turtle— 'for the sake of my life's happiness,' he has told us, 'I dared not make love to my wife'—produced only exasperation. She travelled, acquired a Platonic lover or son in the other Shaw (T. E. Lawrence), hated this house. And there at the other end of the mantelpiece, nine inches high, was Shakespeare himself, too pretty for mocking. I couldn't help picking him up, wondering as I did so whether in four hundred years' time another would be doing the same with a Shaw statuette. Over a chair back, as if just put off, lay a Chinese gown and cap.

Used he to wear it? we inquired.

Oh yes, a gift from the author of *Lady Precious Stream*: their photographs were in the scrap-book. Would we step this way to see the scrap-book?

Another cool, light, angular room looking on the garden—the dining-room—with a mantelpiece of deities, Gandhi, Trotsky, Lenin, Stalin, Ibsen, William Morris— and who's this clean-shaven?—Granville Barker. 'You look at the scrap-book,' I whispered to my wife, 'I'll take a walk round the garden.' At the moment there was a sharp hail shower, but it passed and the caretaker and I set off along curved paths.

We came to trees, steps where the ground fell away. 'St. Joan,' said my guide, turning. None other, gaunt in bronze, one hand clenched and the other shading her eyes as she scanned horizons. I had never much taken to her on the stage. At her feet was buried a household cat. Why wouldn't I, couldn't I, sympathize?

Our path led winding through the trees and the long grass to a small cabin, out of sight of the house. Here, and not in posterity's den, he had written the later plays (including *St. Joan*?) and many of those letters to Mrs. Pat—strange, ebullient, cavaliering letters—which Charlotte might always read before posted. I stared at the small table and chair, the bunk, the electric fire, and—no trophies, no effigy of Shaw. As an old man, with the snow round, he would pull the blanket over his head and write . . . For the first time I was stirred.

147

Back in the dining-room Stalin, Gandhi, and Lenin kept a committee eye on visitors, and my wife pointed to Charlie Chaplin in the scrap-book, uneasily smiling with the message 'To the greatest man in the world, what can one say except "Hello"?' Oh lord. And we're all so sick of Shaw; we can't, for the moment anyway, either like, or enjoy disliking, him enough.

The caretaker and his wife were bearing down on us again.

What prospective tenants? I asked.

Oh several—one gentleman that very morning asking to be shown round.

But wouldn't it be horribly expensive to run?

Not with a quiet decent couple to look after things.

Fires, though—added my wife—would cost a small fortune.

Well, we hoped they would find their tenant, the last whole-hearted Shavian, who would shoulder uncomfortabilities and bestow reverence and love where there had been none.

Visit completed, and thanks paid, we chatted more easily in the kitchen. The big range warmed, a clock ticked, there were tea-cups and, high up on the clothes-rack, a robin singing: all day, we were told, he sang, and at dusk would ask to be let out. Almost that now.

We saw him again, as we passed the drawing-room bow, fluttering, and hopping on Shaw's head, waiting for the casement to open. Blithe bird!—Poor, brilliant Shaw, *rara avis!*

Hey Presto!

A GRAND Festival of Magic enveloped the Scala
Theatre. Every night, wands waved, handkerchiefs
blossomed, liquids changed hue, the snipped rope
regained its wholeness, rabbits were lifted by the ears out
of hats, and of course the lady was sawn in half.

When, alack, were they not? A mere thirty years ago—
on the stage. And now no conjuring is complete without
them. Others we can (and at the Scala did) dispense with:
the ghost at the piano, the levitated boy, King Charles's
head. But a scrupulous bisection—instilled in us, after all,
by Euclid—we must have.

The situation has a decided appeal. How they, the ill-
starred pair, may have come to their present pass, what it
signifies, where it leads, we may not of course know; nor
whether it is of regular, even weekly, occurrence. But
supper, we may presume, has passed with small appetite
and few words; the servants have been dismissed for the
evening. The hour strikes. All is prepared. Then how
trustfully, with tender gaze and smile never faltering, will
she submit to the whim of her strange lover; he (the
victim, no doubt, of some Hoffmannesque addiction)
points to the gaping trunk; in she must get; she's tied up;
the door or lid closes, the clasps snap to; and now begins
the ordeal with its pledge—but do we detect anguish in
the lover's face?—of a happy conclusion. Terribly, in a
silence broken by the metallic clang and rasp, the moments

go by; there is an even more dreadful pause when, work done, the hero may perhaps sit mopping his brow; then one by one the instruments of martyrdom are withdrawn, and it's all over. Out she steps, fresh as morning, while the orchestra triumphantly holds a chord—*she*, since one can hardly suppose the roles reversed. For a gentleman, in the circumstances, to enter or leave that trunk into which, with all the ceremony attending a wedding-cake, sabres have been thrust and saws introduced, would bring, even in these days, profound disillusion. No, it is up to her.

Wardrobes are another matter. Better men than I have found them accommodating, and when the wardrobe stands high and dry in a field, serving as the village lock-up—as it did in the resuscitation of Nevil Maskelyne's *Will, the Witch, and the Watchman*—why, anyone might find himself there under a new moon. Sixty or so members of the audience, mostly children, chose to go through first, on a tour of inspection. (A healthy distrust of the furniture would seem the lesson of all these pieces.) Then the wardrobe was locked, the play started. A 'comedy of the year 1750,' it dealt boisterously with a pair of lovers, a gnarled parent, a gooseflesh constable, a witch, a monkey, and hints of the very Devil. One or more of these was always in clink (though never the right one), and what with scampering round and nipping in and never coming out, and a cupboard displayed to us bare as old Mrs. Hubbard's when it should have been crammed, we grew dizzy keeping track of persons and events. The Monkey especially made the most of a very uncertain status, and the whole romp left us wishing that conjurers, who don't have to prove how clever they are, would adhere more to a past in which mystery flourished. Fairies, ghosts, goblins, familiars, poltergeists, and their successors in ectoplasm and cosmic ray, offer surely a richer field of bamboozlement than the silk handkerchief and the helpful cylinder. It seemed to me, as an outsider at these festivities of The Magic Circle, that the magician was letting go of too much. His style grows familiar. He is giving up dread. What he needs is a sound Gothic revival.

However I must admit that the appearance of young Mr. Fred Kaps (World Champion Conjurer, Madrid, 1950) quite upset these reflections. Mr. Kaps is a dandy. He strolls on in evening dress, twirling a cane, lifting an opera-hat, radiating inscrutable ease; the perfect cigarette advertisement. He glances over his newspaper as only the man of fashion, in thrall to horses and women, can, at the same time rolling it faultlessly round his cane, and with some news item about to vanish always catching his eye; then the final corner is smoothed, the stop-press lingered over, and with a gesture—so much till tomorrow!—paper and cane float away in a crumpled ball. No mistaking the fluency, the impeccableness of those fingers. They summon a pack of cards, and the cards dance for them, fly, turn over, stand on end: Kings and Queens start from the atmosphere, to be scattered recklessly. Mr. Kaps smiles, sweeps off his hat. Now he seeks the relief of a cigarette, and the cigarette's his; blows a smoke-cloud, from it detaches a new lit cigarette, flings aside the old, puffs, plucks, again and again. Thin air be damned, he'll rifle it thick! And the orchestra goes on playing soft dance tunes. And Mr. Kaps, smiling, says not a word. Why should he? His fingers, those most eloquent actors, have spoken for him. They have reached the end of their idyll, and the applause storms across. Encore! But all we can bring back now is the smile, the congratulation. A miracle is over. Out of artfulness has sprung art.

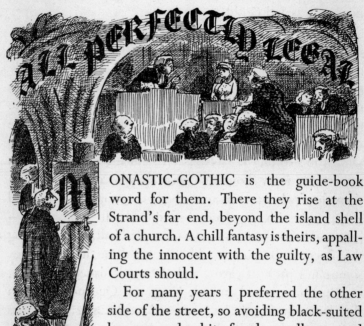

ALL-PERFECTLY LEGAL

MONASTIC-GOTHIC is the guide-book word for them. There they rise at the Strand's far end, beyond the island shell of a church. A chill fantasy is theirs, appalling the innocent with the guilty, as Law Courts should.

For many years I preferred the other side of the street, so avoiding black-suited lawyers and white-faced appellants, and glimpsing the whole without a sensation that it might fall on me. One day I crossed over. It was at a time when I had given up smoking; I was clinging rather to insides of buses, various picture galleries, City churches, the British Museum Reading Room, opera. The Law Courts extended a prim-grim invitation, and I entered.

Even when I had gone back to smoking I continued to

drop in. Punctually at ten o'clock the tower gates, east and west would have opened, the habituals shuffled in. One ascends a long stone spiral—there's a good deal of stone concealing, it is said, thirty-five million bricks; a landing is reached, a corridor stretching eternally, but soon barred off; then the doors to the public gallery. The Court sits.

Sits—somewhat uncomfortably—and doesn't prowl or bob up and down or start up in a fury, as may similar courts elsewhere; and when the time comes—1.30 for lunch, or 4.15 in advance of the rush hour—it will rise. It observes week-ends, and keeps terms—four in the year.

'This *gentleman*,' a lavish voice is proclaiming, 'arranged to meet *another*—not at Dickins and Jones's, or at Debenham and Freebody's—but at Gamages, for *lunch*.' Silk speaking. Had poor homespun in the box so erred? It seems, with bowed head, he had. Even his baldness will tell against him here, where the cranial weaknesses of others are hidden. The judge's plump wig places him in the eighteenth century, as may also some of his observations. Wiglets perch over fat jowls and lean necks. The Portia whose duties are to swear in witnesses and number exhibits is twice as distracting and pretty for her silvery curls.

The court itself is light-panelled and severe, too big for squash though not big enough for *pelota*, and set out with boxes, benches, elevations, and tables. Rules are as precise, if to a visitor unfathomable, as demarcations and styles. Thus everyone, except judge, jury, and officials, sits hard. The Press squeezes into a tiny side pew where a young lady, bolt upright, stares ahead while she plays on the silent typewriter in her lap.

Style is pre-eminent in attack and defence, objection,

insinuation, adjudication. Ermine should be fatherly, even grandfatherly, with a tendency to quips and innocence; silk may sneer, at those who don't pay it, or act the family physician with those who do; time costs dear, and so there's no hurry; the very building has been paid for out of unclaimed moneys in Chancery; everyone will be kept in his place, and justice, as the law sees it, will be done.

The fascination is to watch poor Life, as, by question and answer, it is transmuted to legal fiction. In goes the sad or wicked, multi-coloured event; out comes black and white, suited to the garb of the court.

One may not quite take the finer points, but how loftily, how incontestably an outline is impressed! What could be more judicial than the judge—Lord Goddard, perhaps—who, throned and desked, reduces everything to his own narrative in long-hand, and gives utterance, as he writes, to such strange avowals as 'At that time I was working for Venus and Company of Bond Street'? Would counsel be counsel if goat's hair didn't jig on pink necks? Could any of those volumes behind glass or on desks be *il*-legal, or solicitor's foolscap tied up with yellow, or pews other than painful, or silence sweet, or the jury (should there be one) not wreathed in its own fog, or the person in the box—that shiftless nobody—not guilty to the very boot soles? We cannot but tremble for his mistakes. A goaded 'It wasn't so!' or 'Stop!' on behalf of Life in this unequal match with the Law would produce a stir in the gallery: while we may not applaud, we may—within reason—stir.

We may also—as I discovered when fighting my own battle against tobacco—take snuff, and by so doing catch the judge's eye. It is as well, though, to do this quietly, without any of those winks or grimaces natural to snuff-taking.

Tedium or pity will drive us out in the end to other courts, where other epics, enthralling for the moment, are being drawn out; the will that has brought a family together for the last time, bandleaders who tempt rising counsel to sing in court, embezzlements and arsons, murder itself in the appeal stage, and the sordid conveyor-belt of divorce. 'What's there to cry about?' asks the overworked judge testily. Oh nothing; only dead hopes, and so forth. Life!

And then, to further wandering, are disclosed vaulted passages, mysterious stairs, doors marked Master Grundy and Master Diamond, bridges, dim courtyards, vacuous halls, departments for warrant seekers and regions of the Inland Revenue, a whole geography of 'bear gardens,' 'next door,' and 'over the way,' where a dark but amiable fraternity travel to and fro on errands with their hats on.

Recently I have grown rather bolder in my visits (bad sign!), and now, whenever I find myself down that way, I can't resist dropping in as one might at Lord's, where the procedure is no less exactly odd, timeworn, and oblivious of time. Mustn't miss that last half-hour, with a stubborn defence and the bumpers flying and the court crouching round. Will he do it? Bravo! Ssh. Tomorrow, 10.30.

Here, the other morning, in depths not unlike those of Madame Tussaud's, I took coffee with a barrister friend. All the faces were conspiratorial, gossipy, cheerful.

It's as well to know the ropes.

Some day we too may have to go in at that main entrance in the Strand, and by a fatally natural progress come out at the back to Carey Street.

Sweet Thames

NCE again, from Putney to Mortlake, the river has tasted Spring: faces out in a rush, balconies ablaze, bridges overhung. A cheering wind rounds the corner; meticulously the two eights heave in sight, jerk forward; and waves slop and clap at our feet. It's all over. Blue day, whatever the weather! Six hours later, perhaps, may turn up as good racing for Head of the River, but who cares? What price the London Rowing Club? Londoners will have settled back into the dinginess from which they came.

There may be some sense in it. The theatrical excitement pinned to those few instants leaves us, for the remaining three hundred and sixty-four days, free to enjoy the Thames as we would. And enjoy it, in our obscure fashion, we do. We may no longer (heigh-ho!) sit over Greenwich dinners, and can't, like the gay Parisian, cheat time with a fishing-rod; but we paddle (don't we?) at Tower stairs and moor at Richmond, glimpse St. Paul's over the water, jaunt on Eagles to Southend and fling crusts to the gulls at Blackfriars. Mall and eyot and reach—every appreciable view and squint of the river—are domesticated. And besides, there are the prowlers, and the pickers.

I myself prowl. Whenever in London I have a spare hour, I make for the nearest bridge or embankment. Battersea

Park—what remains of it—enchants: I'd rather there than anywhere idle a noon or engage the smoky-red urban sunset. At dusk the tugs, pulling their three or five barges, lower funnels and scream like elephants at the approach to Vauxhall; swans—or their ghosts, stiff-necked—haunt the dreariest creeks while keeping a sailing dignity; a police-boat bustles; starlings may loop the loop of a bridge-span; and with low tide there's the miscellaneous shore.

At first it may seem uneventful. In Mayhew's time—a hundred years ago—the river would have been busy with beer-sellers, fishers of dabs and eels, dredgermen hovering about a sunk barge or other treasure; into the sewers marched the sewer-hunters, and the shore was thronged with wood-gatherers and metal-finders—old women and children for the most part, brought out by hunger. Today, larders being better stocked, shores are empty. Never quite empty, however. Always a gull or a pigeon picks, a duck remains squatting. And there, solitary, walks a man. Among the green stones and chains, the cans and the tyre cases, what is he looking for?

I had passed by such men, at Lambeth and elsewhere, for years; if I stopped to watch, they found nothing; it seemed a hobby, or avocation, for which they were not uncomfortably rigged. But what was their secret? Not till —strange induction to Thames mud!—I had been keeping tropical fish for eighteen months did I discover it. *Tubifex!*

Tropical fish, I should explain, require warmth and light, and a certain amount of live food. The first one can switch on—with some disturbance to one's quarterly account. Live food is another matter. A garden will provide earthworms, and in most ponds will be found daphnia or water-fleas, fairy shrimps, mosquito larvæ and such. These,

157

creatures of summer, come and go. *Tubifex* stay the year round, but are hard come by—except over a counter. Walk at any time into one of the fifty or so London aquarium stores—where also a boa constrictor, parrots, pert young alligators, and the shy hamster may claim one's affections—and ask for sixpennyworth of *tubifex*; 'tubey,' if you want to seem knowing. The pinch of overstewed rhubarb (as it appears) will be well wrapped in paper; and at home, tipped into a jar of water, it will flower like a sea-anemone. Each frail, inquisitive hair is a worm, extensible to a couple of inches. And so, animated by the drip of a tap, your anemone will live for days, growing smaller as you steal from it.

It's odd, this stimulation of plain water, because the Mud or Sludge Worm, while he may sometimes frequent old pond edges, prefers tidal mud with a seasoning of sewage. The London beaches are his Riviera, and he will choose his spot delicately, neither too near nor too far from what he fancies. To discover his breeding haunts and follow his migrations is a specialist's job.

Such then—and no mere harvester of iron or old tyres— is the lonely figure along the shore. He steps in Wellingtons, and carries a hand shovel, which must be adeptly wielded, a swilling basket, and various tall tins for packing his wares. He may be seen at night, in mid-winter, working by the light of a lantern.

His card announces the 'Dealer in Live Fish Foods, Wholesale and Retail, Supplies Guaranteed.' A new motor-bike is his, a television set on which no doubt he saw more of the Boat Race than I did. He may not have struck gold, but *tubifex*, at threepence to sixpence an . ounce, isn't—as he puts it—to be sniffed at. He has come a long way from Mayhew's beachcomber.

Apocalypse

FOR a month the advertisement had been pointing a finger at me on tube platforms: 'The Heavens are Telling!' See—it went on—the wonders of the universe, the stars filmed through giant telescopes, and Mr. G. E. Vandeman, at the Coliseum on Sunday afternoons, admission free. The first Sunday afternoon I missed, being in bed with a cold. But when the day came round again—that day not only of rest but of deep unenjoyment—I was up and out early, having read in the newspapers of the crowd, five thousand strong, hustling to get in.

Five persons seated on the steps of the Coliseum met my gaze as I descended St. Martin's Lane. They were arguing briskly. 'I don't *see* Him,' remarked one, a small elderly lady with hooks in her eyes.—'No need to,' suggested a smiling Jew.—'There's a mind, of course.'—'Ah, there's a mind. But tell me, how can you have a mind without a body?'—'Oh, quite simply, it seems to me'—'Take yourself, my dear, take yourself!'—'Mind I can cope with,' insisted the lady, biting into a thick sandwich, 'but as for person—you can contact Him, you can't visualize Him!' This she flashed as much to me as to anyone, but I—no sixth man—was already in Trafalgar Square.

Snip-snap went the photographers. A car back-fired and all the pigeons flew round and round Nelson. Why do we go on loving him so? Largely, I imagine, because, though there, he is out of view. I met him face to face in the National Portrait Gallery round the corner (admission free): a pert, fresh, humorous presence, still with two eyes and more than a little of Hogarth's Shrimp Girl. (His Romney beauty nestles next door.) How wistfully come many of the faces—Swift dead, dead in fat; but near him Pope lives, and there's life of a kind—a clown's final appearance—in the painted bust of Colley Cibber. Beau Nash, so waggy, saggy, baggy, pouts a tiny cupid's-bow of a mouth out of a dark corner; the fey foxy Brontës seem trapped in some heavenly thicket. But in every case, is it more the sitter or the artist who holds sway? The equivocation—for after all, on one side or the other, there's more genius confined here than in all the other galleries put together—follows us from room to room, floor to floor. The public, the Sunday-at-large public, was less engrossed than by the pavement chalkings outside. It formed a small circle round one picture: the late King George VI at breakfast with his family.

When I emerged from the Gallery, St. Martin's Lane presented a most orderly queue which I joined. Bad legs were a favourite topic. We were handed leaflets informing us, with an array of texts, that Christ was on his way to rule over Palestine. We were entertained by a cringing Dickensian paper-snipper, and then by an acrobat who turned somersaults and worried himself through hoops: as he stripped to the vest, the rain started. Ah, Sunday! But soon we were waddling in, and the first excitement—choosing your own free seat—was ours. Could I smoke? Apparently not, though some openly munched chocolates. The house quickly filled. 'Last time I was here,' the man next to me confided, 'was for *Annie Get Your Gun.*' He had been disappointed; he wouldn't be so, I hoped politely, today. Old people who looked as if they hadn't been out for a long time were enjoying the advantages of stalls and circle. I heard Italian, French spoken. A baby cried. Two Negroes appeared in an empty stage box and modestly sat at the back, the light gleaming on spectacles and faces as the curtain went up.

What an array of chorus, one hundred ladies in tiers dressed like Puritan angels, and behind them fifty gentlemen with black bow ties and butterfly collars, all ready to burst into a hymn! They sang well. Their plump conductor, quick with the smile of success and such asides as 'Praise His Wonder,' sang also in a clear tenor and got us to sing: one verse from the circle, the next from the stalls. Then to an oversweet tune the choir were chanting.

'The light of the Cross, the light of the Cross Shines through . . .'

and shine at that moment it did, in red electric bulbs from the back of the stage, while the footlights dimmed and three missioners slipped into three augustly waiting chairs. There was a prayer, all standing, followed quickly by the collection; and now at last, spot-lighted, it was Mr. Vandeman's turn—he who questions us from the advertisement. Like the other two, he was clad in black, but escaped their odour of shop sanctity.

First, in pleasantly transatlantic accents, he warmed an audience disposed to be knobby and sluggish. We were in a muddle, seeking, seeking, and we must look up. What should we see? Had the universe fallen into order by itself? A Chicago business man, no believer, had remarked, 'Well it may be chance, but all I know is that if the parts of a hatchet were shaken up in a cloth for a million years they'd never make a hatchet.' This brought a pleased murmur. Five angels, their turn over, appeared in the front of the box, with the two Negroes peering between their heads.

Some astronomical figures started the ball rolling, or the worlds turning: Betelgeuse 120 times (was it?) larger than the earth, the sun's flames reaching out 500,000 miles, and so on. The sun, in fact, brought a flush to cheeks as did once, if less benevolently, hell fire. Lantern slides caught for us this flame-headed giant, somehow imparting a woolly enthusiasm which the 'film' advertised might have missed. Bedazzlement was Mr. Vandeman's means. He turned over millions, he dealt in immensity, allowing himself one wild trope when, after dangling before us the bright confusion of Orion, he suggested that there we might find the gates of the Heaven of Heavens. The wand pointed; the Bible was ruffled through for a text. Did the left hand know what the right did? We—the audience or congregation—shifted like overfed diners, and sighed; we had sipped the wine of enlightenment, we were flattered that all things should be, enormously, just so. A benediction, a vote of thanks, a reminder that next week ('Are Other Worlds Inhabited?') would astound even more, and we were on our way out into a wet yellowy twilight that gave no indication of the heavens that, at a touch, had opened.

Better Times

HEN people talk Utopian—
   'Steaks for all!'
   'Down with trousers!'
   'One language, one oppor-
tunity, one world!'
   'Open Joanna Southcott's box!'
   'Who's for Outer Space?' etc.
—when they roar or sigh for Utopia, which they don't as much as they used to, I think of mine.

It doesn't fly off, can't compete. Quite simply it's there; or was this morning, and will be tomorrow.

*   *   *   *

The pale dawn seems to antedate man. I've been aware of it off and on before I get up, and now moving about the house, opening windows, putting a kettle on, I meet its blank stare.

It is very blank; as am I, though not with the same assurance. We gaze, sky and I.

Divine dullness, enlighten me; depression, raise me up!

Won't the kettle—indolent, snuffling brute—ever boil?

*   *   *   *

Years later, sipping my first cup, I regret the impatience that has driven me, as usual, to snatch at this milky-violet concoction, hot to the throat. But the second cup will be good char.

A rook caws, flaps over. Two rooks. They sweep away remnants of the night, bats and such: mine continue to play a little.

Now if ever, between times, I'll have glimmerings. The world, the big day lie ahead like some concert platform on which one by one the performers arrive, establish themselves, flourish instruments, lick lips and flutter fingers, ready to begin. They converse, they tune up . . . up . . . With the descent of the baton and the opening bars my private enlightenment ends.

*   *   *   *

A lark gets up. The spider, having worked, rests. The enchantment he has worked about my gate will be broken by the first-comer, the postman; and then he'll go spinning again, like a successful novelist, till lunch.

*   *   *   *

I had almost forgotten the quiet sky, grown incontrollably brighter, and now blossoming pink, yellow, and purple. Suddenly, the topmost branch opposite is lit with gold.

Out of the east, too, have come shadowless gardens, suburban dolls'-houses, telegraph wires, the mildly-inquiring snail, and my fifth cup of tea—all, of course, with sugar and milk added.

But surely even this cigarette—Western though it is—spindling away, fits the picture?

A cat. *My* cat. Except that at this hour he's not mine, and if he looks this way it's through ceremonious slits. He sits under a rose-tree, listening.

*   *   *   *

Birds sing. What do they sing? We no more know or care than in opera. They sing.

Some of them not too well, either.

*   *   *   *

I have been listening for a sound that would certainly not be caught if it weren't expected: that of a motor-bike free-wheeling downhill. Every morning this visitant will glide past—there!—standing and paying attention to the gardens and at ease despite his goggle-suit. He might be a well-disposed if gigantic insect, but is, in fact—hardly less surprising—a Korean with a landscape-gardening connection near the railway. Often I miss his free passage, to be jogged by the stutter of his engine when he reaches the bottom of the hill. The significance of his country's name, he told me once when we met on a crowded platform, is 'Morning Calm.'

*   *   *   *

Sunlight reaches my tea-tray (seventh cup: warm-up), and the paper on which I am writing. Thus early, I don't recognize that while one may start the day with genius, one goes out as a hack. So what I write shines too.

Cats have no problems of self-expression. There are two of them now, aslant to each other, and a third, I suspect, up the yew. They practice magnetism. They lie in wait. They are.

All at once, but with no change of attitude, they stiffen. What, who can it be?

Round the gate-post comes wet india-rubber, a nose. One eye. Good heavens—dog!

Time must be getting on, then!

The nervous peep—no more. The cat party he can't possibly see, since they're well under the hedge, but he and they have exchanged recognizances.

He slowly withdraws, and then trots by in full view as if nothing had happened, or could possibly happen.

One cat yawns.

*　　*　　*　　*

Things, as a matter of fact, are beginning to move in all directions. A boy with a satchel has come running to thrust in a newspaper next door; an aeroplane of an old type makes its vacuum-cleaner drone; trains creep like snails; there's an indefinable over-the-hill mutter that's London.

Hard boots ring out on the pavement—a workman, with a hat but no tie; followed soon after by a black-coat with tie but no hat, and soft feet. He seems rather less possessed by the dignity of labour than the other.

A convent bell rings. Typists rush out of gates. School-children with bouquets and acid-drop voices loiter as if they had a whole lifetime before them. Everywhere lights and shadows, hurryings, stresses, movements in space and time begin a criss-cross; and for the first time I become aware of the clock's beat—that heart outside one's own that always needs looking to.

*　　*　　*　　*

And that really ends Utopia. The post and the press floor me; rather than weep over things, I grin in the shaving mirror; I dress up; I step out; and the day's mine, sunlit at the moment, though I'll be lucky if I can free-wheel it like the Korean.

166

Of course, I've forgotten something and have to go back.

On my second exit I meet the dog, Hugo by name, who now guards his gate, quite at his ease. His lip curls when he sees me. But he doesn't bite. He's unhappy. Perhaps he's off bones, or in love with a cat: it may happen. Distantly we nod to one another with the one meaning we share in common. It's a dog's life.

Animal Spirits

THE London Zoo has recently celebrated its hundred and twenty-fifth anniversary. It has come quite a long way. A small triangle in the wilds has pushed through tunnels under road and over canal to become a big triangle, and now from the bison to the brush turkey is a tidy step. Seats just not sticky with new orange and yellow, licks of paint here and slaps of whitewash there, a grand avenue of flags have marked the occasion, which is being spread over the year.

But at once from these mild festivities we are distracted. The peacock, the peacock is strutting!

He spreads himself in a fine old Persian manner, never having heard of Iran or oil. The Moussadek writhe would be a vanity unknown to him, and presumably also he hasn't read his own designation of 'Common Peafowl, Male.' Uncommon surely he may claim to be, as, outsparkling the featheriest goddess of the Moulin Rouge, he advances and recedes, side-steps to reveal the musical clacking of wings sacrificed to fashion, shudders with melodramatic appeal, and is all eyes, as indeed are we.

Only the hen remains uninfluenced: a bit overdone, she seems to be saying, as she pecks over the gravel without even glancing up. There's a whole terrace of these exquisites, a Princes' Row, and one and all they are airing their tails and taking a squint to see how the other fellow gets on with his, or executing a sort of knock-kneed dance of rage up and down the netting. More shining even than they, the white peacock has been situated in a distant pheasantry.

Elsewhere, if never so gorgeously, a spring fancy touches Creation. The black-coated penguins are waddling out from a banquet, and the hyena rolls on his back: he'll die of laughing, before ever he comes to that joke. Then, how goes it with the giraffe? Still a bit governessy, condescending? And the baboon blushing? Has the lion given up dreaming of unicorns? Does the eagle frown, and the hare cringe, and the gorilla hold out a begging palm? So many old familiar faces! All we require is the assurance, sometimes odd and delightful, sometimes alarming, that they're as they were, and that an old world remains. We may change our spots, not the leopard. No shift of policy is discernible, under the lens, in the ant-city, at this moment excited by a gift of orange slices.

The news from Korea is of leopards, larks, humming-birds, otters.

Poor *Homo sapiens*, he has such a burden to slough off! As one dawdles a way round, it's as well not to linger with those who too insistently hold up the mirror—various monkeys and apes, for example. Tropical birds and fishes will plunge us into a world more of art than of life; and I have a fondness myself for the Small Mammals house and the Rodents and New Arrivals. The latter especially exert a lively lure for the curious. Genets and porcupines, treeclimbers, burrowers of one kind and another abound; the unlabelled tarsier (or is it a loris?) with headlamp eyes delicately haunts; and we'd warm no doubt to the Least Chipmunk, if he didn't so observe the disembodiment of his name.

A strangely cloaked, amicable group is that of the Indian fruit bats, clinging (one with its baby) to the roof, trembling, blinking in the diffused sun. The railing across the corner is for their protection; last year one of them died from cigarette burns. They don't resent, and seem hardly to notice, inquiring fingers. An umbrella wing is stretched as though to illustrate kinship with the pterodactyl. Two hooks serve for hands, and the attitudes are mild, surprised, uncertain—and of course, upside-down.

Upside-down also, in the next cage, is the sloth pacing to and fro aloft, watched incredulously by a small armadillo (pre-history has certainly set foot here). Our own world being already so—topsy-turvy, I mean—we can sympathize with the point of view, though its voluntary assumption remains mysterious. There, how thoughts, more than bars, intrude! Can't we look at anything, even Zoo animals, with fresh eyes? The bother is that, if we rid ourselves of our own troubles, we may tend to assume theirs. Some are pretty well off, others not. In too many cages squats the bugbear Boredom. The flying squirrel, safe but grounded, bats hemmed in cubicles measurable by inches—what twilight ever is theirs?

On the other hand, give them wing-room, and away will zigzag fun, interest, sympathy, and the rest.

So it doesn't do to stay overlong. I enjoy a portrait here, a pat there; and soon I am ready to go out where I came in. But what's happening in Princes' Row? Such a hullabaloo! The birds squawk. A little four-foot elephant, passing with his keeper, has gone almost mad with pleasure. He won't be dragged on. He must squawk too. Then he barks; and before this unexpected admirer the peacocks outvie one another in their fan-dance which looks like going on for ever.

One thing, by the way, since this is a gala year, and visitors from abroad are expected by the thousand. The Zoo is well supplied with cafés, but in not one of them will you obtain a cup of coffee.

Roller Derby

WHAT could it be? Steamrollers? Men in sacks, gee-gees on wheels? But really to find out, one would have to make the journey to Harringay, where, with hockey as the usual call, the ice has been broken.

On a fine evening, then, I emerged from the tube blinking to find myself in one of those long streets that seem miles away and yet in the thick of it, and up which till recently trams had ploughed. On one side was urban disfigurement; on the other, park railings, through which after a while I spied cricketers. A very white boot was advanced; ball met bat and dropped dead; one laundered figure strolled to pick up the ball, which was tossed to another, who dollied it to a third. Irresistible, to anyone who has shared in them, these lilies and languors!

Already in the big echoing hall a dozen skaters—ah, roller-skating!—men and girls sportively stripped, were sauntering, weaving, swooping, and even prancing, all on wheels, round the pale-blue rectangular track, curved and banked at the ends. Dance music played at elephants in the roof. The arena was spot-lit, leaving us shadowed, so that I could make little of the rules and procedure minutely retailed by the programme. But from the scattering of stars and stripes and an indefinable swagger, this must be America.

Europe—a Europe, apparently, owing allegiance to the

Union Jack—took its place. Now an audience swarmed in, wolf-calls and whistles greeted favourites, and the elephantine music gave way to a mammoth *Voice*, so shaggy and huge that, while it incited us throughout the evening, it may well have been with recitations from *Also Sprach Zarathustra* in the original.

What then happened had to be, by me, gradually picked up, though everyone else, I may say, seemed thoroughly at home. The two teams ran loose, coalesced. Round and round, like that thirtyish tune, they went. A pack would form; a whistle would blow; faster and faster they'd spin, more climactic would grow the voice; and then one racer, seeming to tread glue along the straights and taking the curves at a swoop, would streak or struggle ahead. If within ninety seconds he could overtake adversaries in the pack, his side would amass points. Then another stroll-round, another jam, an exchange of women for men, and so on.

It had been done, after the First War, on bicycles. From the patience of the trenches had emerged the marathon dancer, the pole-squatter, and the Six Days' Cycle Race, with the racers working in pairs to gain laps; no time signals and no horse-play: and in the hinterland of the track those resting slept in bunks, ate, read, took showers and massage.

The centre space now confines itself to an austerity of team pews, penalty boxes and, most conspicuous, a raised stretcher or operating table. The significance of this soon appears. Skaters in a jam are permitted to obstruct, barge, hustle, and with their elbows knock flying an opponent. So much the rules (which I have had time to study since) encourage. But the rules aren't everything. Sooner or later helmets will be flung to trip, chopper blows will rain in the neck. Feuds start on the track, to develop into free fights off.

'We want the Ref.!' chants the crowd in unison, 'we want the Ref.!'

Don't, in the cause of law and order, join in this. It will turn out otherwise. One skater with a grievance will first push and then give the Referee his straight left. The crowd has asked for the Ref.: they get him, laid out. Vast is enthusiasm.

And all this in as many moments as, I suppose, it has taken one of those batsmen across the way, hearing the bails fly, to walk sorrowfully back by the way he has come.

It battered, it began to grip me. During the interval I circled the corridors, pushed through gum-chewing crushes round doors marked 'Gentlemen Skaters' and 'Lady Skaters,' passed a supporters' Den (strangely empty), washed down a leathery sausage-roll with red tea, and listened to a boy of nine arguing with one of eight about the integrity of one Toughie, the stockiest, swiftest, most howl-provoking blonde on the American side.

The second half of the evening repeated the first, varying men's and women's bouts, show-downs with the Ref., an open-house pursuit in which with fine gestures a scarf held in the teeth is snatched one from the other as the leadership changes. There is grace as well as skill in the quick, ceaseless roundabout, and the antics of a skater hopping or gradually losing balance over twenty-five yards can be gratifying indeed. What would a Roller Derby be without favourites floored? Or a real Derby for that matter?

Has it come to stay? Perhaps, so long as fun, dash, noise, the tinge of violence, and the enthusiasm of fans who afterwards take the track, keep the turnstiles clicking.

Of course, it's not cricket.

Southend Fling

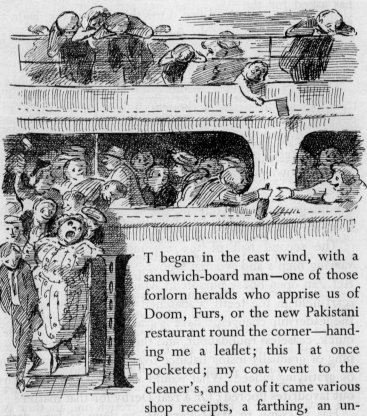

IT began in the east wind, with a sandwich-board man—one of those forlorn heralds who apprise us of Doom, Furs, or the new Pakistani restaurant round the corner—handing me a leaflet; this I at once pocketed; my coat went to the cleaner's, and out of it came various shop receipts, a farthing, an unknown button and the forgotten leaflet.

'Eagle Steamers!' I read, smoothing it out: 'Day Cruises to the Sea from Tower Pier'—drawbridges

lifting, in the photograph, before a shining new vessel—
'to Southend, Margate, and Clacton; Weather and other
circumstances permitting.'

My last visit to Southend had been—Munich permitting
—in 1938, when there were little Chamberlain brollymen
in the sweetshops, and the sunset gave awful promise of
destruction.

Well, the waters had flowed to and fro since then.
Thames had been set on fire. One thing, however, hadn't
changed: dep. 9 a.m. Oh! But at 9.1 bars will fly open;
and this miracle, quite as much as the sniff of sea, draws
bona-fide travellers from their beds by the thousand.

That very Saturday I would go! 'Impossible,' said the
travel agent, of whom I thought it best to inquire, 'all
booked up.' So, with the edge off impulse, it had to be
the next Saturday.

And there I was, long before 9 a.m.—how hard in the
circumstances not to be *too* early!—with heaven knows
how many others, wandering down over the cobbles,
squeezing between parked charabancs, dodging cars and
kiosks, linked arms, fish-porters looking like damp peons.
A taxi or two. Fat woman pleading with officials for her
fat pug. But what says No. 6 of Important Notes? 'No
dogs are carried.' Damning the universe, a great dray
drawn by chestnuts charged uphill under the lowering sky.

'You can just as well get wet here,' said the beefeater
to his small attendance for the Children's Beach.

Our own queue zigzagged away down to a floating quay.
On board every staircase and corridor were jammed by
two factions slowly fighting a way through one another as
in halma. Youths with an accordion (despite '9. No
musical instruments') were camped by a bar; somewhere
a hen party had begun to clack and dance. Will you,

won't you, *won't* you join the—An immaculate gentleman, wearing a vest-slip, appeared, and the way seemed to open before him.

There was less commotion on deck, where the seats were already taken: I was lucky to share a bench with three tailors, who talked among themselves unintelligibly, but with their hands to the rest of us. It had struck nine long ago; and then amazingly, with a couple of snorts (six would have meant she was heeling over) and the bridge elevating as in the picture, we were off.

Pale ale! But before the first could froth over, a Voice took charge, bid us good morning (shrugs from the tailors), embraced the riverscape, called on Mr. Boyle's party to proceed to the forward dining saloon for breakfast, coughed, and put on a gramophone record.

'My Baby Loves Me,' as Greenwich, noble and deserted, slid into view, followed by Woolwich, Erith, and Silvertown—all seemingly stricken by the explosion of the last—and so past the maiden liner *Ostrava* and a cluster of sail barges to long bare river walls broken by an occasional village or factory. Here Good Queen Bess yelled 'I know I have the body of a weak and feeble woman,' there pylons out-topped St. Paul's Cathedral.

We didn't miss much, and it all had a Stygian charm, enhanced by the atmospheric blight that seemed endemic.

To the throb of the engines, breakfast followed breakfast (but where, now, were the *remaining* members of Mr. Boyle's party?), beer chased beer, and the crowd had begun to get the measure of itself. We were gay in spots. We drank from bottles, and surreptitiously felt for sandwiches: spectators of fun rather than fun ourselves; two thousand of us from the Home Counties, as it might be at the Ideal Home Exhibition or panto on ice.

The river spread out, losing the Kent coast, and in a haze we were touched by the blank surmise of *Outward Bound*. Hours late, should we ever see Southend? Bottles flew overboard. A chorus welled up: 'Mother Brown,' followed surprisingly by 'O come, all ye faithful.' Two teddy-boys waffled past, short of stature and trouser, but long-coated and long-haired. A gimlet of a woman, with tiny grey topper askew, danced a jig. The immaculate gentleman was seen on the captain's bridge, raising binoculars: a waiter ran up to him, and he drank off what could only be—the gesture asserted—a stiff whisky.

Then the end of the mile-long pier loomed ahead, and we all started shoving our way downstairs. When we emerged it was a new blue-and-white day.

Southend is a fun-fair and a parade for the paper-hatted —with sombreros, bobby's helmets, and jockey's caps much fancied—and the crawl to and fro along the pier and a bobbing of boats and a mud-flattery and cockles and giggly postcards and open-top buses and 'Torture through the Ages' and the tide bringing back the icecream cartons, and four hours of it was just enough.

The boat might be late (and was, by an hour), but not so the gangs, the families, the coach parties and the couples, swarming back to make their long, long queue.

The immaculate stranger watched our embarkation with the interest of one who has done the full trip to Margate, Clacton, and the open sea, and perhaps availed himself of the telephone service on board (10/6 to any part of the British Isles). A glass of whisky in hand bespoke continuity.

Cheerier all round was the way home, with circles growing and voices raised in song *against* the loudspeaker, 'My Darling Clementine,' 'Mademoiselle from Armenteers,' and 'Don't have any more, Mrs. More'—all those female old contemptibles who assail the Cockney at dusk. Beer and stout flowed; high tea (up to 9/6, with lobster) tempted some, gin others; silhouettes brought the shore near; lights wriggled; we were tired, but it was a tiredness sweetly drawn out. All the time I couldn't help feeling I had lost something—pocket book, pen, key-ring . . . myself . . .

It was dark and quiet when we glided again under the upraised bridge to find—oh so unreal, unexpected and beautiful!—the Tower lit up; and rather sadly, as the decks were being swept of our rubbish, the bottles piled, we melted away in the gloom of a hill famous for execution and riot.

Wisley

W E had been mushroom-picking. Not the orthodox kind, but small flat yellowish mushrooms, and fried in a little beef dripping they tasted delicious. Of course, before shaking them into the pan, we had looked them up. 'There you are,' I said, spreading open the chart bought once—now was its first testing—from a chemist in Lyons, '*Clytocype géotrope.*' 'No,' said she, pointing elsewhere, '*Amenite encymée.*' Either, neither; with perhaps a touch of *Mousseron.* However, since none of these at all resembled the four death's-heads blackly sequestered, we didn't worry.

They had caught our eye on Wisley common as we meandered away from the Royal Horticultural Society's gardens. Few who attend Chelsea know Wisley: there the shop window, here the private address. These three hundred-odd acres in Surrey have more than room for the trickle of sightseers who on a fine day, leaving any accoutrements at the lodge, enjoy walks and woods. One shouldn't, to look at flowers, be crowded; nor should the flowers. Loudness ill becomes them. They are attending an Edwardian garden party. That 'naturalness' we so take to is, of course, as artificial as any other style. Nature left to itself knows no rock gardens, no herbaceous borders, no svelte lawns, no elegant climbers or creepers that learn when to leave off, no pine shade under which grows cyclamen, no fairway up a hillside, no clumped shrubs and orderly woods. All these are the product of an art at least as self-cognisant as that which plotted Versailles, and to our minds more becoming; the artists have borne names like Robinson, and have joined native sap to a sometimes horrible phraseology. The Garden Beautiful meant, in fact, beautiful gardens. Wisley is one. (A Wilson played his part here.) In any month of the year it reconciles the pleasures of, say, Kenwood and Kew: no great house, but no strict botany lesson either.

It was new to us picking our way and discovering views without probing them, then exploring part of the rockery. This last, an acre of hillside, has hidden to the ascending eye its network of paths: tweedy ladies rose out of some giant bog-plant, an open-shirted young man fancied a pinnacle, gentian sparks with the blue-green of distant sunbirds had chained to the spot an undertaker (so from his costume he seemed); there was a runnel of water to be traced past basins and falls, and woods to look back on. And notebooks, pencils, without which there would be no Latinical shopping lists. Something gay, small, fresh starts out of the rock: chalk it down! I had myself collected, on backs of envelopes, *erodium chamaedryoiedes* (pink flowers) and *convolvulus mauritanicus* (pale blue). A visit to the doctor couldn't have more enhanced me.

We talked to the superintendent, as at home as a rock lizard; and to the old gardener who, with the help of a girl student, manages—bottoms up—to keep this hard acre in trim. We inquired the price of muscats, sniffed stocks, stared into lily-ponds, trod the lawns framed with pretty pink and white daisies. We loitered along the herbaceous walk, a broad grass path with borders of Robinsonian splendour rising to high hedges. We drank the cup of tea provided from a caravan in a neighbouring field (oh Jones, or whoever it is!). We discovered a large, and it was claimed appetizing, fruit crossed between orange and mandarin; and soon, far too soon, the clock pointed to going home. It was on our way (curvaceous road by Brown, clouds by Constable) to the roaring Portsmouth Road, that we saw the mushrooms: greedy fingers, at which seed-pods had been nodding all the afternoon, couldn't resist them.

*   *   *   *

Second visit. Determined to step out and see all we've missed—lakes, orchards, heath gardens, formal gardens, pine walks, rosaries, flower and vegetable trials, etc. Large bag for mushrooms, together with chart, so that we shall know from the beginning what we're about.

Wisley itself passes in a sunny hallucination, from which we remember leaves dropping, crimson montbretia, a quince by a lake, the sixty-yard herbaceous walk waiting to be cut into a jigsaw, and serve-yourself at the caravan, with wasps queueing.

On the way back we look out for *cêpes*—those large greenish-brown mushrooms whose fleshy strips the French relish with garlic and parsley. What's more, we find them. Enough for a meal for six, together with smaller (and we decide, harmless) odds and ends variously tinted.

Look of horror on the face of the Green Line conductor at what he sees peeping out of the bag.

We aren't so sure ourselves when, at home, we regard our pickings, washed, cut, seasoned, frizzling, and almost identified, half a saucepanful. They smell sweet, but look sluggish. I peruse in Charpentier all the descriptions and comparative tables; so little divides succulence from poison, life from death; everything, it occurs to me, may hang on a colour-printing process not too fine in its shades. Some of the saucepan's contents are going mushy: wrong! As a final resort I lug out the *Encyclopaedia Britannica*, which after informing me that the species of fungi number 100,000, flies away to this strain: 'In the Oomycetes, homothallism is the rule (except *Dictyuchus*), and the gametangia are clearly differentiated into antheridia and oogonia.' At any other time, this would fascinate me.

We look at our piled plates. The cat sniffs.

'Delicious,' I suggest.

'Then you try it first—only a little bit.'

I taste. I wait. A faraway train hoots. There's the least aftertaste of—of—

My hesitation is enough. The mushrooms are bundled away in a newspaper, to be buried deep where the cat won't find them. We nibble mutton-and-mint-sauce sandwiches. I read a little of Ivanov on Dostoevsky. Next morning I wake with a headache, but it wears off.

It may have been, that morsel, *comestible*; it may have been *douteux*, even *véneneux*. We're where we started. Such vagueness, I know, won't do if we're to be selective mushroom eaters. But with no glowing native tradition to light us—no mycologist Smith—we feel rather lost. Better stick to flowers? That vision of a pale-yellow late-flowering clematis at Wisley, what matter if it's labelled this or that, and if for some it looks pink with spots?

Green Thoughts

I DROPPED in on a billiards match the other day. That sounds casual, but in fact for some time I'd been waiting the chance. Snooker we have always on view, billiards rarely. I suppose the war scotched it. Matches that never went on for less than a fortnight diminished in appeal when one's next night might be one's last; and today the eye no longer darts, or darts vainly, to the stop-press or the foot, the very bootsole, of the column for 'Latest Scores.' The twilight newspaper passes over Mr. Davis's 439 unfinished. Tempos have changed; we prefer the quick decision, the knock-out.

However, once in a blue moon the billiard players, those guardians of misspent youth, come back. Spry, black-suited men, imperturbable as comedians, they have

184

stepped in through curtains, bowed to the empty house, inclined together at the baulk end for stringing (one moment during this ceremonious conflict when they will act in concert), and after their fashion they're off. Not that I—or, I imagine anyone else—can ever have been present at such an initiation. Billiards matches start and finish in heaven. Did not Lindrum once make a break of 4,137? Who saw, who could possibly see, that? Has there ever been a champion who didn't threaten to go on for ever, so that new rules had to be devised—spot strokes barred, three cushion cannons made obligatory—so as to check him? Don't the victors of all time, Walter Lindrum and John Roberts, Jr., Peall, Gray, go on playing one another irresistibly, even though in the game's present eclipse we may not hear of it? One walks past that old-fashioned façade in Leicester Square, the 'Home of Billiards and Snooker,' with no more thought to the immensities than along lamplit pavements under the night sky. No shooting star or onrushing planet—in the shape of a smother of glass, a ball flying out of a first-floor window to bounce at our feet—reminds us of the strange universe within. Only, if one happens to glance sideways, the scores are put up beside a doorway.

So I dropped in; and already as I was mounting the stairs, galleried with cartoons of famous players, came the voice of the marker: 'One hundred and one . . . three . . . seven . . . nine . . .' Then curtains divided, I was admitted —held on the threshold—to the hush, the green radiance, the performance, the music of the spheres click-clicking their journey through eternity.

A confident, snub personage in shirt-sleeves, whom I recognized as Mr. Joe Davis, was addressing the ball. He dealt with it briefly, scrupulously: others may be over-

polite, suspicious, coaxing—not Mr. Davis. He simply
addresses it; it does what he wants. It nudged, and no
more than nudged, the other two balls, and so they went
on sidling almost imperceptibly until Mr. Davis paused,
raised an eye-brow, and away went the ball round the
table in a series of smart rebounds, while Mr. Davis
watched to make sure it wouldn't deviate by a hair's
breadth from some course previously decided on. It
didn't dare. It slowed down as much as it possibly could;
its two companions, huddling together, waited; Mr.
Davis waited, we all waited; and with an incredible
reluctance it came back, nearer and nearer, so close in the
end that the marker had to bend over, shading his eyes, to
decide whether all three weren't touching. This enabled
me to find my way, on tiptoe, to a seat in the fourth row,
four rows on either side steeply banked being the limits
assigned to gods and men.

The session continued as such sessions do: cigar smoke
thickened to pyramids over the enchanted green; the
score leapt up and the clockhand crawled round; from
time to time, unaccountably, Mr. Davis went and his
place was taken by Mr. Willie Smith, a genial elder and
ex-champion of the 'thirties, less strict in his surveillance
than the master; a purr of content from the front row
would sharpen into gasps, slaps of astonishment at the
back; a lady plumped in, secure in her satisfaction of
being unique; and to the marker's intonation was added
the clubman's snore.

My own enjoyment on these occasions always takes a
similar course. At first I tremble for every stroke, amazed
that in the pursuit of intricacies success should so follow
success: to anyone who has ever wielded a cue—as I did,
for many years and many purposes, having been brought

186

up, as you might say, on a quarter-size table—the spectacle
sublimely discourages, revealing as it does the gulf
between pottering about and playing. Then, with miracles
rattled off three to the minute, my amazement reserves
itself for the shot that *doesn't* come off, the ball left hung
on a lip. Finally, between despair and elation, I acquiesce,
I accept, I relax, I lose myself in a perfection that may lull
but never dulls. Green thoughts under a green shade. The
players cease to exert themselves in expunging error, the
strokes merge into impulses, impulses into a break, and
the spherical three—more golden than those which hang
outside Uncle's—attain their own heaven of communi-
cability.

After the hour of billiards, refreshed as though by
midsummer streams or the Turkish Baths, we sat up for
the now indispensable lapse into a half-dozen frames of
snooker. Snooker is a devilish short, sharp gambol. Of
course, being masters of every style, Messrs. Davis and
Smith—the first, a long-reigned snooker champion—
brought elegance to dodging, and showed off delightedly.
The click-click had became bang-bang, the epic had given
way to the strip cartoon, and we had all been thoroughly
tickled before we felt for hats. Our small crowd dispersed
grinning, but outside I looked back for that reassurance of
the calendar:

W. Smith (rec. 3,000) 6,148
J. Davis (in play) 7,823.

Torso of an All-in Wrestler

TO discover him now you must journey to the ends of the earth: to the more remote baths, that's to say, the dockland cinema, the Palais on a night off. There, as an alternative to dogs and speedway, he can still pack a hall; and, sucking ice-creams and wooed at intervals by dance airs, the audience will mildly admire, gently remonstrate. But mildness and gentleness are not his aura; he needs the hissing, cat-calling, laughing multitude. Where are they? Not at the Wimbledon Palais on Thursday nights. Riot (that release we go on calling un-

English) has taken other ways and fashions. On them, on him, respectability of a kind has descended.

Very different were the acceptances when, in the 'thirties, he first came to town. (He has grandchildren, by the way, who delight year by year in his Father Christmas.) Then the West End—the sporting West End—was his. Most weeks would find him at the Ring or at Lane's Club. Ugly or handsome, he looked the part, and acted up to his looks. He started doing things. He gave us our first taste of violence: one that afterwards we were to cultivate most lovingly. Not that the discovery had been his. Gorillas were padding the sidewalks of Chicago, and in a Munich beer-vault conspiracy had raised its head with a scowl. But these were far-off, indeterminate shadows. At home we knew rather better. So long as gentlemen walked out through their gate at Lord's, and the sun (more or less) shone, and Englishness mattered, and to every sport could be affixed the word 'noble,' what had the world to fear? Into this arena of lost causes barged the all-in wrestler—no respecter of persons: he grunted, he belaboured, he hugged, he gouged, he flung, he tied in knots, he unravelled, he all but murdered and was murdered. No highbrow either; boxers might dote on Shakespeare, not he. On so many stages Beauty had posed for us, that this late arrival of the Beast seemed a necessary completion. This was what, in our dreams, the Windmill girl had been waiting for; and before we could get over our first shock of astonishment, pleasure, and disgust, he had turned the ring itself into a stage, bringing the audience closer than the most popular comedian.

The Ring, Blackfriars—in good theatrical, bear-baiting country, and intended originally by the Rev. Rowland Hill as a chapel with no corners in which the devil could

hide—was his true home. Elsewhere, like Hitler in
Copenhagen, he might behave; at the Ring he was
delightedly, furiously himself. His audience rose to him,
playing a part incidental to his. He would toy with an arm
or a leg: 'Break it off!' they advised. 'Make a ballet dancer
of him!' and 'Heave, heave!' (sometimes to the tune of the
Volga Boatman) were other favourite calls. And talented
members of the audience acquired distinct roles. There
was the deep bass voice at the back that never failed at an
early stage to liven events with a hortatory 'Open up them
pearly gates!' (It took me some little time to discover
what these were.) There was Warmed-up Death, so
denominated by the crowd, a lady of surprisingly pale,
thin aspect, with a tight mouth and an endless cigarette
holder, who, never smiling, never missing an evening,
occupied a front-row chair; and others, some remarking
and some remarked upon, who weren't slow to underline
the love-knot parody of the whole thing. Our traditional
view of sex as ugly and comic found here some frank
embodiments to add to the pantomime dame and the
music-hall harpy. The *poses plastiques* of the ring, accompanied by such barks, wails, kisses, and cries of 'Oh,
mother!' as matched the situation, would have delighted
moralists and painters in an age of satire. Hogarth might
have devised yet another Progress, beginning on a nursery
floor and ending with divorce from a princess. For
though reputedly ill-paid as he was certainly hard-used,
our hero had his opportunities of fame and success in the
great world.

Play-acting forged so important a link between con-
testants and audience that subsidiary dramas arose. A
wrestler might get out of hand, threatening havoc; he
might even—like the bull jumping the fence at a *corrida*—

turn and rend a critic. There was always that possibility, to add spice to repartee. It rarely came about, but when it did the occasion was notable. I shall never forget that evening—not, as it happens, at the Ring, but at Lane's Club in Baker Street—when the Terrible Turk broke loose. He, a bald bearded giant, was fronting an opponent no less terrible, and in fact was so much getting the worst of it that he found himself, after being spun round and round above the other's head, hurled headlong out of the ring—a drop, I suppose, of ten feet. For a moment he lay dazed at the feet, so it chanced, of a very drunk gentleman. He—the drunk—woke; beheld the dejected Turk; cracked him smartly—and in the true *esprit d'alcool*—on the head with a bottle. This had the effect on the giant that sol volatile might have on you or me. He sprang to his feet. He bellowed. He would have clutched his assailant's throat, but that the other, wonderfully sobered, was already away down the aisle and flying out through the doors. The Terrible Turk followed. We all followed. And the last that was seen of either—that night, anyhow—was two figures, one in evening dress, the other naked, disappearing into the lamplit distance of Baker Street.

Of course, it may all have been prearranged, though I hardly think so; divine accident is not so easily simulated, and the times encouraged it.

Nothing of the sort 'marred the proceedings' when, a couple of Thursdays ago, I followed out an old weakness to the Wimbledon Palais. A gimlet-eyed woman knitted in the front row—good start; the bouts were crisp, varied; low comedy was provided by the 'extra-special heavy-weight return clash' between the Shipyards' Strong Boy and The Russian Tearaway (hairless, in black tights); 'Ugh, ugh!' they huffed, and the pleasurable 'Ah!' would

191

slowly change to 'Oh!' and then 'Oh, no, no, no, no!'—
the classic reversal and height of eloquence at these
encounters; but the onlookers no longer howl, the referee
wasn't once sandwiched, and my impression was that
within the ropes they kept more to the rules and that
there were more rules to keep. Much of the time the
audience might have been attending—but for some lack of
intellectuality—a performance of the Brahms Requiem.
Gone the bold buskers, the anguished peace-maker, the
furious intimacy of the ring, gone the Terrible Turk; and
Death—she, I believe, may be no longer Warmed-Up.

On the placards I see old familiar faces—Jack Pye,
George St. Clair Gregory, Harry Rabin; and I wonder
whether, apart from the added twenty years, they are
quite themselves. Haven't we de-terrorized them? Over
their beds, to which they retire sober and early, does there
hang a gilt-edged text of the rules? Is the beast tamed?
One and all, have they bowed the head, submitted, to
fair play? I dread to think so.

S O it is called; and there they are, fifty or more of them, big, bright birds cluttering the shore.

Beautiful, at this moment,

they are not; no swan that respects legend would ever come out of water till after dark. If its top half belongs to ballet, what of the lower? Policemen in nightshirts have been mentioned in this connection. I am sure Leda never met hers walking.

However, here in the evening sun they seem determined to show everything, preening themselves, waddling, scratching under one wing. Good-bye, violins. Welcome, social security. It's the old story.

The wedge of rubbly beach where they have gathered separates two huddles of boats, houseboats of a miscellaneous order, among which are barges and landing-craft, a couple of small yachts, a floating dock, a ribbed hulk, all (with the exception of the last) conditioned for living. It is high tide; the boats sway gently, groan, nudge one another, and a passing tug will impart agitation. 'Chelsea Yacht Club' is the name on the biggest craft, which seems to combine the offices of porter's lodge and estate management.

If for the swans the struggle is over, the shore gained, the human inhabitants of the reach have won no such victory. Money has walked in at one end of Chelsea, and they've popped out at the other: so at least, from a distance, I've always assumed. But Chelsea carries so many drifts, what with painters and pensioners, china shepherdesses, buns, traditional losses at football, an arts ball, and a flower show—heaven knows what else—a physic garden—that I may well be wrong. I have never been one to plant roses round an old bus or find equilibrium in a windmill, and no doubt I underrate the urban life afloat.

A year or two ago I was introduced to a barge-home in The Hague, a model of Dutch tidiness, with a water square almost to itself, but with everything (including a nursery and a dark-room, the owner being a photographer with children) so fitting with everything else that a step from one room to another involved Cox-and-Box exchanges of the furniture. I admired. I was horrified. Such permutations were not for me. My Dutch acquaintance, a widower, seemed to find consolation in the tight embrace of his new home.

Once even, in the ditch days after the war, I looked into a houseboat at Kingston-on-Thames: fortunately the price —£3,000—and some confusion over sewage and a bathers' paradise nearby rendered the idea fantastic.

However, Chelsea has had stronger claims. (That swan, now, stumping up to others in conference—whom does it remind one of? The late Ernest Bevin, surely!) It was always a dream of mine to live on the river—on meaning, for this purpose, beside. Everywhere I listened for the tugs, and after a hard day I'd hurry down to one of the bridges for a blow. Pope's grotto at Twickenham, with its camera obscura, brought the flowing waters on to his very walls—what an idea that was! Such a cinema would be mine also; I'd incarcerate Thames; switching on the light, if not to seashells, then to the appurtenances of a sitting-room in Southwark or Pimlico. It had to be at the hub; the more vast and unbeautiful London grows the more a real Londoner wants to be held fast. And what else, like the river, can soften our urbanity and open skies wide? Once or more a week I enjoy making the walk— which leaves the riverside only a couple of times—from Blackfriars to Chelsea. I have never found, at my price, the Thames-endowed flat I'm looking for, but it exercises my affections. I have got to know my scene in all its climates and moods, the tugs pulling their train crabwise under bridges, hayloads in the fog, swans nosing their way along wharves, Nine Elms yard and Battersea Power Station, the beautiful sad Embankment lamps strung to infinity. On the

Embankment, no doubt, I shall end—no, I'm forgetting, that's frowned on today.

And now—when it may be too late—I am about to board this floating hamlet within a crow's view of Charing Cross. 'For Sale' notices catch my eye. I cross the deck of the 'Chelsea Yacht Club,' grasp a rail—none too confidently—and step on the next boat; and so from deck to deck, rail to rail, making my way to the landing-craft where I'm invited.

It's a snug light cabin down steps, with a tiny stove, a window seat, a wall table at which my hostess has been busy painting and dressing little plaster statues of cavalry. I am warned against putting the sherry decanter on the mantelpiece; there may be a tug, silent for once, passing. 'Diz,' who is with me, goes up on deck to sketch the swans which are almost next door.

Have they names? No, just 'the swans,' like 'the chickens.' You feed them, but no egg for breakfast, no roast swan on Sundays.

I learnt that the boat, converted, cost £600, and a first floor could be added for another hundred; fees, to the Chelsea Yacht Club, £5 a month all-in; two rooms, kitchen, and bathroom; main electric, telephone hoped for; handy-man to cart off refuse, etc.; tank filled every day with fresh water; no rates to pay, and an address in Cheyne Row.

'I'd much rather live *there*, of course,' adds our hostess, nodding shoreward.

There is quite a charm in the easy rocking, the clack of waves, glimpses and sounds of the river. Once, I am told, they all woke up to find they'd drifted into mid-stream. Everyone knows everyone else: medical students, a painter of the view upstream, a mysterious Hungarian with an infant, a talented young star of stage and screen, and two of the 'politically-conscious' who spring out when one passes, exclaiming 'Quiet! baby asleep!' For good or bad they're lulled together, tilted and then lulled again by the tides.

The snags seem to be feeling your way in the dark, shovelling snow off the roof, pumping out (once a month) the bilgewater which condenses everywhere if you try to get up a fug. Summer's the time, and Sunday the day.

I am tempted, though not very seriously, as I might have been at twenty-five.

'Diz' comes in, feeling the cold, and saying he'll have to pay another visit. The gang-planks interest him.

'They terrify me,' I say.

It's getting late, and we climb on deck. And there at last, gliding, all in white, stage-lit, frowning on their reflections, are three swans. Dear, dirty river, how could I ever live without you? But *with* you—impossible!

Round and Round, Up and Up

E has all but run up the seventy-foot mast, to discover a swaying platform not three feet square. Just the thing: after a look round he stands on his head, levitates himself sideways, arches back. So much would appear routine, the unfurling of a human flag responsive to whimsical breezes. Our applause never fails to waft him, a cobweb on the ceiling, in some new direction.

Every afternoon and evening renews these gambols. The circus is back. Whips snap, spotlights reach higher, horses interlace to a music never quite theirs, elephants hold tails, clowns lament, riders burst through paper hoops, the sea-lion has magnetized his nose, and the lions look sorry, though not more than we for them. Round and round it goes, up and up. And at Harringay—where will be found Arnold's, the best circus I've seen since the war—all eyes were fixed upon No. 15.

His flutterings, his projections this way and that must have almost exhausted themselves, when out of nowhere descends a chair. It will suit his pedestal nicely. But first, can't chairs be stood on their hind legs? No sooner purposed than done, he himself on top of all, to preserve the balance, realizing a hand-stand (as I believe it's called) or hair-raising perpendicularity. So, upside down, to his satisfaction if not ours, he floats. We applaud, fearfully. A bad moment, but won't it pass? Yes, with the arrival of a second chair.

If only, with a wave, we could banish him, disentangle ourselves, revert to any among the precedent numbers! Irretrievable, now, is the calm of 14, a 'Majestic Mixed Group of Tigers and Lions' in which one tiger would always be sidling off to lick at the lion next-door; and No. 13, those 'whirling, twisting, turning somersaulting,' but earth-bound acrobats, have been woven into tapestry. Then there were two gorillas, most life-like, who contented themselves with buckets of water and simple pole-climbs, one of them, when the heads were flung back, unmasking a woman. The sixth sea-lion as usual, playing truant, had got more than his share of herrings, but displayed a more than usual expertise in balancing lighted lamps while slithering up and down step-ladders. The elephant, sadly, had danced. Why? Even Milton, adumbrating the first circus, let him off with a writhing of the lithe proboscis: now he must hunch shoulders, shuffle feet, and make a final appearance in evening dress. Surely we have comedians enough without thrusting risibility on the most august of animals? The clowns, as it happens, are especially rich in variety and numbers, having a vast playground outside the ring in which to unroll eternities of sleeve, go fishing, enact bull-fights, and take the dog (poodle-headed at both ends) for a run: here Death bicycled past, with his pal behind, two skeletons on a mission; possibly the sick lady on the couch, that seems languidly to perambulate itself, required them; they're too quick for her, racing on to claim with a grin a lanky, striped individual enjoying his first bathe of the season.

But the dreadful Now abolishes Then. The employment of the second chair grows urgent. He—ex-Olympic champion Tell Teigen—has decided there's no choice but to stack it on the first—squarely set—as waiters do towards closing time; except that here, with insinuations and leanings that nowise exaggerate the delicacy of the situation, the disposer must accommodate himself on what he disposes. Consider that! The chair slips—*his* little joke, in case we aren't interested. Then, just as we're resigning ourselves to the second chair—which has acquired a decided wobble—comes a third. We cannot but look, daren't groan, hesitate to clap. Our heads remain prayerfully lifted. Yet what prayer can we utter? That he should come down? How can he come down, when to do so means dislodging his sole means of support?

One of the clowns I remember to have come upon a similar problem *ambulando*, the heel of one boot pinning the other toe; the more he struggled to take a next step, the more self-rooted he became; then the lights went out, and even that solution was denied us. A favourite moment, by the way, with painters: the company of clowns and augustes disporting itself—and what's a clown but Papa, or oneself with grief and ailments coming on?—when suddenly the light is put out, the spotlights point, there's an entry of heroes or beasts, and the new act (or display, to use the preferred term) is sighted over a chiaroscuro of clowns in flight, one still twirling overhead a plate on a walking-stick. Harringay has the advantage that its circus wholly occupies the building, with no distraction of light or sound from adjacent funfairs, menageries, etc., so that the darkness here expunges, the hush can be felt: two essentials if any circus is to be itself and not a mere round-about of acts. Ideally the circus should be round, high, close, breeding familiarity and wonder.

Already—heaven-sent like the others—a *fourth* chair has alighted to join the ascending three; Teigen is still—only he knows how—on top. 'No net!' whispers indignantly a lady nearby—'disgraceful!' What about regulations? But on with the net, off with the act. Dread, which has flown out of the wild-beast cages—every trainer now negligently turning his back—rules the height. The very best act of the evening has been (at thirty feet or so) the beautiful Pinito Del Oro who, without loss of grace, takes the swinging trapeze unsupported on her head, while her partner waits open-armed below. Where would the circus be without risk? Bedazzlement, fun, wonder—yes, but danger is the brandy that sets alight.

And at last, despite everything, he—our thumbscrew Icarus—has managed to unchair himself and come down: young, handsome, dapper, a trifle pink from his exertions.

A fellow-journalist (I note retrospectively) writes with enviable sang-froid, or in obedience to his calling, of a *fifth* chair. Such there may be, though I didn't see it. Or perhaps the number varies according to the aerialist's form and mood, with afternoons when a mere three must satisfy, evenings of surrender, of triumph when he will soar into double figures . . . the while outside, dogs yawn at doorways, and an old woman makes much of negotiating the kerb.

At St. Pancras

ONLY ten minutes to go; but in ten minutes everything will crowd round. It takes a moment or two for the dusk—here it is always dusk—to lighten, for place to impress itself. People are catching or missing trains, looking for trains, waiting for trains. I have to meet the 2.3 from Derby; out of fogs and snows (what a country!), she is on time. (Well then, thank God I'm not a Spaniard!) 'Have we time for a cup of tea?' asks a sad, thin girl; and 'Nice time,' replies her man—not all time, you will observe, or no time. I've nice time to look round; and most reassuring do I find the atmosphere of promptness without hurry, confusion without panic, and discomfort that lulls rather than gnaws. Three men are trying to get a racehorse into a van. Do they go mad? Does the horse? No.

Every Londoner, it is said, has his station, as he has his dog or his newspaper. Mine is St. Pancras. Not that, more than once in five or six years, I use it for travel. But I meet trains. I drop in, or should I say pay visits? So high it stands, so inviolate, its pinnacles lost in cloud or touched by a sunlight no longer ours, palace by nature and terminus by necessity—surely some Antipope or Caliph or Kane has fallen on hard times. But to the street below there's no hint of fall, of perhaps the distasteful business of engines. Superb over the black abasement of King's Cross rise its eastern extremities, with a lady among the spires whose identity can scarcely be guessed at; the west end,

only less majestic, overstares the muddle of Euston; a
massive centre tower emphasizes a chief portal. As we
ascend nearer, a thousand Gothic windows, reputed once
to belong to hotel bedrooms, look down.

We pass through. Faint as last week's cigar smoke
comes the aroma of sulphur and dust, dung and damp.
Although trains don't obtrude, there's one near. Its
engine pants with a thrilling metallic timbre that causes
another, far off, to give a little scream or gasp; but nothing
more comes of it. It is a mere interchange of nature. They
are getting a little restive, perhaps, and will have to be let
out or separated. Has anyone here a train to *catch*? It
doesn't appear so; trains do in the end come and go, and at
the correct hour, and people get in or out of them; but at
their leisure, as though the train had been waiting for them.

Lord's itself couldn't be more pleasant to idle in, the
benches outside the Refreshment Room indeed suggesting
the enclosure there. Quite a number of people sit enjoying
the scene. Different tactics have been tried with the racehorse, such as pretending to pay no attention, and hoping
that curiosity will finally lead him to investigate a coach
furnished to resemble a horse-box; but even from here
one can distinguish that the supposed backside of another
horse within is of painted wood. A very few passengers are
getting down from a three-coach local. A tweed-suited
gent affronts the bookstall and, having reviewed the
photographs in a shiny weekly, with a decided 'No!'
strides away, moustache bristling, to the telegraph office;
he is followed by a very small lady who surreptitiously
asks, and pays, for *The Handweaver and Spinner*. The
parcels platform is—considering the season—decently
vacant. There are no runnings to and fro, no late-comers
pounding on gates, no breakings through queues, no

shrieks or whistles, no dreadful Voice whispering unmentionable places. And everything is contained under one
vault, open at the end to such an estuary of sunlight and
steam, overhead signals, clouds, a seagull or two, a
delicate gasometer clump, as Monet never envisioned on
the Seine. Railway for railway's sake!

And then, just as the post-lunch enchantment is ours,
a fat fellow comes barging along, hands in pockets, cap
pulled over eyes, goose if you please under arm, and
—this we can hardly believe—an illuminated tie; a
tartan bow, that's to say, lit from within, that flashes
off and on as he walks. What *can* he be doing here? The
thought must suddenly have occurred to him also, for he
halts (the tie, of course, switching off), turns round, and
exclaims with a laugh that he must be in the wrong
station. That has already been to us painfully obvious.
Probably he's a King's Crossite. One gets to know the
various types: Paddingtonians are owlish, Victorians
flashy, Eustonites grim, Fenchurchmen frankly peculiar.
The Pancratist can be recognized by a hat slightly taller
than the ordinary, a withdrawn look as though the world
were already sighing over its Great Days of Steam, its
lost lines, vanished cathedral-stations. Sometimes, when
actually travelling, you will see him scrupulously walk the
length of a train, as though in search of the second class
compartment no longer his.

The 2.3 comes in at 2.3, I discover my cousin, take her
arm, seize her bag, but with thoughts elsewhere. Shall I
one day be admitted to full Pancrasy? Room with a clover-
leaf window? House at Luton, straw hat to tilt all summer
as I travel up and down?

A neigh. The racehorse has won this time. He is being
led off.

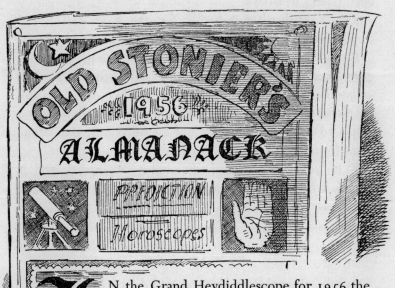

IN the Grand Heydiddlescope for 1956 the heavenly body Cow will jump over the sign Moon, with Fork and Spoon in elopement, and amazing results in science, sport, and song. Unenjoyment will pass away, and the £ Sterling will make a new challenge to those who fiddle it. Voices will rise and fall, stags will chase bears, bears hug bulls, a seven-leafed clover will affect the whole destiny of the British Isles, the first sky platform will appear over Harrogate, giving rise to confusion in parties at home and in the House, there will be new hope for tram-lovers, and the weather will start conversations, though this will be offset by crimes of exceptional brilliance.

205

Electricity concerns may receive a shock from the quarter they least expect.

Hair will continue to fall, and, in some circles, stand on end. Those under the influence of Rum should avoid ladders and fretwork.

The Kabbalistic number o for the year will be of importance to all who fill in their football pools on Friday.

From Mars—once so far away—will come reports of grave consequence: governments overthrown, nations embroiled, arguments over Peace leading to War; the development of the kink-bomb, imparting a destructive ripple to space waves, must not be ruled out. But vibrations from Venus promise better.

Keep your eyes crossed (concludes Tea-leaves), and it will be a year of effort and success for everyone, including postmen.

BEWARE OF

DISGUSTING IMITATIONS

Note.—The Prophetic Writings for the months (which follow) rend the veil with more than usual thoroughness since we have secured the services of a noted oneirologist who, following the Dunne method of dream prevision, has spent the last year studying the newspapers of the year to come.

January

A wave of good resolutions sweeps the country. Share-pushers begin to recite poetry, poets pay income-tax. Cigarette-smokers are tempted to give up smoking and take to Morris-dancing instead. The Dog being in chine with Lollipops, this movement has a fair chance of success, and a republic is declared in Streatham.

Good year for whist drives, which should, however, open quietly.

February

Mr. Aneurin Bevan leads a dance of congratulation to Sir Winston Churchill on the occasion of his thousandth hat.

Good time for unfreezing pipes.

Sow winds and discord.

March

Trousers will be worn short this spring.

Sibelius finishes his eighth symphony, and this is followed by news that the L.C.C., which has been debating ways and means of improving the London traffic situation, will begin by pulling down St. Paul's.

Nathaniel Gubbins joins *The Times*.

April

While horse-racing may get flatter, winners will be both expected and unexpected, and punters are advised to plunge carefully.

Stunning attack on Wolverhampton widow. Disgraceful, says magistrate, the season doesn't start for at least a fortnight.

May

Peer Assaults Bus-conductor: Gave me Punch: But Couldn't Read. Uproar in Court.

June

The Sun is issuing out of Pickleparsnip, and women will be admitted to the Stock Exchange and the Guards.
King Monolulu crowned.

July

More friendly overtures are promised at the Festival Hall to inaugurate a new era of international concord.
Kinsey report on horses banned in Kensington.
Compulsory attendance at Battersea Pleasure Gardens.

August

Club-man Expires in Window: Bored to Death: Foul Play? Club Rules Silent.
Film star walks off screen; absent-minded; silly season, anyway.
Those born on the 12th will wish they never had been.

September

Oysters and crumpets in season. Well-known Q.C. dies of a surfeit.
Mr. T. S. Eliot's new comedy, *A Remarkably High Tea*, is generally acclaimed 'the perfect scream.'
Reap fruits of victory, whirlwinds, etc.

October

The Mona Lisa's smile vanishes from the Louvre. Where is it? Renovation blamed. Possibility of gang at work. Are Cromwell's warts safe? Big reward.
Stalin seen at Cesarewitch.
Moon enters Barbican. Keep indoors.

November

House of Commons burnt down. One-line Hansard. Question to be asked. Winnie's cigar? Reported offer, I'll lay first brick.

Fog covers the land. New novel by Mr. Charles Morgan.

December

Mr. Gilbert Harding to play Peter Pan.

Buy your Old Stonier's Almanack for next year, refusing all ghastly imitations.

Mona Lisa smile will be found by Press photographer illuminating the features of Mr. Evelyn Waugh as he steps out into St. James's. He cannot conceive how it got there and is much annoyed. It will be removed and returned to its rightful owner, but this may involve delicate operations.

Bathing in the Serpentine.

Year drowned in bells, including first wrong number.

STRANGER, PAUSE

S O high are walls, it might be a prison (there's one not far off), but under them one reaches a drive-in, an arch, a porter who doesn't raise eyes from his newspaper: Kensal Green Cemetery.

If we pause, not certain which way to take, it may be with the feeling that we've no business here, and that when we have it's likely to be out of our hands; also we are realizing that make-believe by which, with some old painting or illustration, we would one day *enter* to look round, dip over the hill, and push the gate to the locked garden. Many times, I suppose, I must have passed this same scene framed by the archway. Now I am in and, pausing, part of the picture.

By luck—for there is more than one entrance—we have come in at the beginning (1835, or so). How beautifully time works, rubbing away what's too plain, and scribbling round and over with wildness! More, surely, than the century has obliterated names; here a couple of head-stones lean together, there a great black box like a side-board has been tipped and left; the broken column breaks, and on sculptural ivy climbs the living ivy.

But if the trees grow and breathe, stone—often in a most curious voice—speaks. Sometimes it may be only with granitic name and date; sometimes an address, a flourish, a text will be added; there will be a wife and children, or a plurality of wives; more than this— information or exhortation of whatever kind—will incline us to spell out what's written. Thus may we encounter Samuel Laver (1797–1868), 'musician, painter, and novelist,' and surely not otherwise.

Sir William Casement, of the Bengal Army, has regi-mented four sepoys (or vikings?) who bear on their heads in perpetuity the canopy of his entombment. Honours abound. William Blake, Esq., M.C.P., will not fail to catch the eye. Baronets, benefactors, M.P.s, captains of war or industry, presidents of societies, all seem understandably reluctant to leave a position. But in this matter of worldly emphasis, who has the advantage— they or we?

One may well ask, since the proud rich man—despite camels and needles' eyes—doesn't, it would appear, go out a whit less rich or proud. Kensal Green may be, as the delighted Chesterton saw it, a remote junction to Paradise, but for many of its occupants Fame or Annals is more

what they had in mind. Last thoughts must remain
hidden; but why not, in every cemetery office, a
tabulation of Last Words, which the visitor might
inspect for 1s. or 2s. 6d., going, of course, to upkeep?
Those in stone too often betray the relative, hiding or
gaining much.

Of disapprobation even the mildest there seems none.
Here praise and self-praise link hands, point the toe, set
off.

'It is the fate of most men
To have many enemies and few friends.
This monumental pile
Is not intended to mark the career
But to show
How much its inhabitant was respected
By those who knew his worth
And the benefits
Derived from his remedial discovery.
He is now at rest
And far beyond the praise and censure
Of this world.
Stranger, as you respect this
receptacle for the dead
(As one of many that will rest here)
Read the name of
JOHN SAINT JOHN LONG
Without comment.'

So, remedial discoveries notwithstanding, it turns out.
And yellow and red burns the sycamore, and a train
passes.

Even those we do know, or think we know, may be
somewhat disguised—Cruikshank, for example:

'For thirty years
a Total Abstainer and ardent
pioneer and champion
by pencil, word, and pen of
Universal Abstinence
from all intoxicating drinks.'

The head surmounting this declaration challenges us in bronze: here (claims *Baedeker*) he is. Here he *was*, Universal Abstinence (or some other cause) having removed him to St. Paul's.

But Leech, Hood, Trollope, Thackeray, the brothers Brunel, Wilkie Collins, and 'James' Barry (first woman surgeon and army officer, who went as a man) are here, in opposition to that other older brigade, the Highgate hill-siders, who include George Eliot, Herbert Spencer, Marx, and Old Mother Shipton. Dickens nicely distributes his favours, having there a wife, and here a ghost-love—Mary Scott Hogarth.

Between the two famous burial-lands has been split also one of the few great myths of the century: that which strove heroically to unite the Fifth Duke of Portland and Mr. T. C. Druce, shop-keeper of Baker Street, in a single person. Only the latter's uncoffining on the northern heights, after fifteen years' litigation, served to quell fancy. The Fifth Duke was all that a duke might be, habitually wearing three suits, one inside the other, tying his trousers with string, constructing vast subterranean palaces on his Welbeck estate and sacking any of the five hundred men employed who saluted him, travelling in a heavily curtained coach drawn by six small ponies, and eating—in two halves—a chicken a day. He was generally credited with harbouring a corpse on the roof of his

London house: this proved—when investigated by a
sanitary inspector—not to be the case. The roof-top was
bare. But the vault of the Druces, which should have been,
wasn't. Profound was the disillusion of thousands for
whom it had become an article of faith that only the Duke,
popping on beards and indulging in midnight rides and
mock funerals, could possibly have run their favourite
emporium.

While I am considering this most delectable of histories
—a Balzac novel in real life—peering through trefoils and
following round inscriptions, an official comes up to
ask if I'm looking for something. 'Yes,' I reply, 'the Fifth
Duke of Portland.' 'This way.' I tell him some of the
story. He points: three hundred square feet of ground,
wildly shrubbed, with relations in a corner. The stone,
of plain granite, is almost flush with the ground; one can
understand, from his Welbeck habits, that he would take
to earth as a duck to water. 'Is there any considerable
system of earthworks or tunnellings?' 'Not so far as we've
heard.' 'No way out, no escape-route to the canal?'
'Definitely not: we should certainly know of it if there
were . . . Brick vault,' he adds.

And there it rests. There presumably *he* rests. Though it
is still permissible, I trust, to wonder whether the boot
hasn't been on the wrong foot all along; beards may be
put off as well as on; perhaps it was a clean-shaven Druce
who whistled up through the night to Nottinghamshire to
lay new plans for catacombs.

After the Duke's enclosure one reaches a more ordered,
less distracting modernity of services and lives rendered,
and then the meadow as yet untouched, with Surrey hills
in the background. For a moment we are in the country;
then turn, walk a few steps, and a veritable Alcazar of

gasworks ascends, catching gleams in the mist and towering to pure sunlight. The place teems with such Follies. This one imposes at the particular instant when we discover what seems to be Compton-Burnett ground: all uncles jostling nieces, and such names as Sabina and Ivy.

In the distance I catch a glimpse of raw earth, close-packed tumuli, flowers fresh and faded. A young woman accompanied by two children bends over a watering-can.

Then, upon us, and upon all round us, there bursts a quite blood-curdling shriek of high intensity, that might be some preternatural summons, a new war, or the Fifth Duke sallying out from his long confinement; but is, in fact—as it discloses itself, with shriek joining shriek to form a sustained chord or chorus—no less than the gas-town signal to knock off. I, too, must go.

Once again the dog sleeps on in stone and his master's love, leaf-smoke drifts over the path, a bird's foot patters on gravel. There have been in these seventy acres forty thousand graves dug and filled. All is numbered, winding and odd—quiet, but not dead quiet.

THE END